Justin McCarthy

✦

HISTORICAL ASSOCIATION OF IRELAND

LIFE AND TIMES

NEW SERIES

General Editor: Ciaran Brady

Now available
Michael Davitt by Carla King
Thomas Kettle by Senia Pašeta
John Mitchel by James Quinn
Denis Guiney by Peter Costello
Frank Ryan by Fearghal McGarry
William Martin Murphy by Thomas J. Morrissey, SJ

Titles are in preparation on Sir Edward Carson,
Joseph McGrath, James Clarence Mangan
and Maria Edgeworth.

Justin McCarthy

EUGENE J. DOYLE

✦

Published on behalf of
the Historical Association of Ireland
by

UNIVERSITY COLLEGE DUBLIN PRESS
Preas Choláiste Ollscoile Bhaile Átha Cliath
2012

First published 1996 on behalf of the
Historical Association of Ireland by Dundalgan Press, Dundalk
This Second Edition first published 2012 on behalf of the
Historical Association of Ireland by
University College Dublin Press

ISBN 978-1-906359-68-3
ISSN 2009-1397

University College Dublin Press
Newman House, 86 St Stephen's Green
Dublin 2, Ireland
www.ucdpress.ie

Cataloguing in Publication data available from the British Library

Typeset in Scotland in Ehrhardt by Seton-Burberry
Text design by Lyn Davies
Printed in Scotland on acid-free paper by
Bell & Bain Ltd., Glasgow

CONTENTS

FOREWORD

Originally conceived over a decade ago to place the lives of leading figures in Irish history against the background of new research on the problems and conditions of their times and modern assessments of their historical significance, the Historical Association of Ireland Life and Times series enjoyed remarkable popularity and success. A second series has now been planned in association with UCD Press in a new format and with fuller scholarly apparatus. Encouraged by the reception given to the earlier series, the volumes in the new series will be expressly designed to be of particular help to students preparing for the Leaving Certificate, for GCE Advanced Level and for undergraduate history courses, as well as appealing to the happily insatiable appetite for new views of Irish history among the general public.

CIARAN BRADY
Historical Association of Ireland

PREFACE

I should like to thank Barbara Mennell and Noelle Moran of UCD Press for inviting me to write the second edition of this biography of Justin McCarthy. I should also like to acknowledge my continuing gratitude to Alvin Jackson, now of Edinburgh University, and Gerard Doyle, for their constructive criticism of drafts of the first edition. Ciaran Brady, of Trinity College Dublin, has been a pleasure to work with on both editions.

Marie Altzinger's editorial skills have transformed this book – as her presence has so many other areas of my life. Joe Carthy, of the College of Science, University College Dublin, a true scholarly ecumenist, promptly came to the assistance of the humanities when I needed an electronic copy of the first edition of this book. Damian Dalton, of the same university, and Pauline O'Connor, also kindly provided technical assistance at short notice. I am also grateful to W. J. Mc Cormack for his work on the index. Any errors that may remain throughout are my responsibility alone.

Research for this book was carried out in the National Library of Ireland, the British Library, The National Archives (Kew), and in the library of University College Dublin. I am grateful to the staff of these institutions, and to the Director and Trustees of the National Library, to the Trustees of the British Library, and to The National Archives, for permission to quote from papers in their respective collections.

Our family of three was recently joined by a small, generous, ambitious, erudite, bearded, bespectacled, determined and deceased

Irishman. In appreciation of her wide-ranging assis- tance, enthusiastic encouragement, and good grace during Justin McCarthy's
disruptive sojourn, I dedicate this book to our wonderful daughter,
Xavière Altzinger.

EUGENE J. DOYLE
14 February 2012

ABBREVIATIONS

BL	British Library
MP	Member of Parliament
NLI	National Library of Ireland
QC	Queen's Counsel
TNA	The National Archives (Kew)

Vincent Brooks Day & Son, Lith.

'Irish history' by 'Spy'

Vanity Fair, 23 May 1885

CHRONOLOGY OF McCARTHY'S LIFE AND TIMES

1830
22 November: Justin McCarthy born in Cork; Earl Grey (Whig) appointed Prime Minister.

1837
20 June: Death of King William IV; accession of Queen Victoria.

1841
30 August: First issue of *Cork Examiner*.

1845
September: Beginning of Great Famine.

1848
September–October: McCarthy reports for *Cork Examiner* on trials of Young Ireland leaders William Smith O'Brien, Thomas Francis Meagher et al. at Clonmel.

1852
4 December: McCarthy joins Commission on Fairs and Markets as secretary.

1853
24 September: First issue of *Northern Daily Times* (Liverpool) – McCarthy employed as a reporter.

1855
27 March: Marriage of McCarthy and Charlotte Allman (Macclesfield).

1856

30 September: Birth of Justin Huntly McCarthy (Liverpool).

1858

17 March: James Stephens founds in Dublin a secret organisation, later known as the Irish Republican Brotherhood (IRB).

1859

7 July: Birth of Charlotte Ely McCarthy (Liverpool).

1860

January: McCarthy starts work with *Morning Star* (London).

1861

January: McCarthy becomes foreign editor of *Morning Star*.
12 April: Start of American Civil War.

1864

3 March: Death of Michael Francis McCarthy (Cork).

1865

26 April: End of American Civil War.
11 May: Death of Ellen McCarthy (London).
June: McCarthy becomes editor of *Morning Star*.

1867

5–6 March: Fenian rising near Dublin.
23 November: 'Manchester Martyrs' executed.

1868

27 February: Benjamin Disraeli (Conservative) appointed Prime Minister for first time.
8 September: McCarthys leave England for first visit to United States.
3 December: William Ewart Gladstone (Liberal) appointed Prime Minister for first time.

1869
26 July: Irish Church Act disestablishes and partly disendows Church of
   Ireland.

1870
19 May: Isaac Butt launches Home Rule movement in Dublin.

1871
7 June: McCarthys return to England.

1872
18 July: Ballot Act introduces secret voting.

1874
February: General election – 59 Home Rulers returned.
20 February: Disraeli appointed Prime Minister for second time.

1878
First two volumes of McCarthy's *A History of Our Own Times* published.

1879
4 April: McCarthy elected MP for County Longford.
5 May: Death of Isaac Butt.
15 August: Death of Charlotte McCarthy.
21 October: Irish National Land League established.

1880
March–April: General election – 61 Home Rulers returned.
1 April: McCarthy re-elected MP for County Longford.
23 April: Gladstone appointed Prime Minister for second time.
17 May: Parnell elected chairman of Irish Party.
27 December: McCarthy elected vice-chairman of Irish Party.

1881
13 October: Parnell imprisoned in Kilmainham jail.

1882

2 May: Kilmainham 'Treaty'; Parnell released from jail.

6 May: Lord Frederick Cavendish and Thomas Henry Burke assassinated in Phoenix Park.

17 October: Irish National League established.

1884

6 December: Representation of the People Act – Irish electorate increases from 226,000 to 738,000.

1885

23 June: Marquess of Salisbury (Conservative) appointed Prime Minister for first time.

November–December: General election – in Ireland, 85 Irish Party, 16 Conservative, and two independent Conservative candidates returned to parliament.

26 November: McCarthy loses Londonderry City election.

2 December: McCarthy elected MP for North Longford.

1886

1 February: Gladstone appointed Prime Minister for third time.

8 April: First Home Rule Bill introduced into House of Commons.

7 June: Home Rule Bill rejected by Commons.

July: General election – in Ireland, 85 Irish Party, 16 Unionist, and two Liberal Unionist candidates returned to parliament.

5 July: McCarthy loses Londonderry City election, but later awarded seat on petition.

8 July: McCarthy re-elected MP for North Longford (does not take seat).

25 July: Salisbury appointed Prime Minister for second time.

September: McCarthy starts tour of North America.

23 October: Plan of Campaign launched.

1887

7 March: *The Times* begins 'Parnellism and Crime' series.

18 March: McCarthy takes seat for Londonderry City.

1888

June–November: Irish Exhibition in London – McCarthy on Executive Committee.

1889

24 December: Captain William O'Shea files petition for divorce, citing Parnell as co-respondent.

1890

17 November: O'Shea granted a decree *nisi*.
25 November: Parnell re-elected chairman of Irish Party.
1–6 December: Committee Room 15 meetings.
6 December: McCarthy elected chairman of Irish Party, following split in party.

1891

7 March: First issue of *National Press*.
10 March: Irish National Federation established, with McCarthy as president.
6 October: Death of Parnell.

1892

July: General election – in Ireland, 71 Irish Party, 19 Unionist, nine Parnellite, and four Liberal Unionist candidates returned to parliament.
7 July: McCarthy loses Londonderry City election.
15 July: McCarthy elected MP for North Longford.
15 August: Gladstone appointed Prime Minister for fourth time.

1893

13 February: Second Home Rule Bill introduced into House of Commons.
31 July: Inaugural meeting of Gaelic League.
1 September: Home Rule Bill passed by House of Commons.
8 September: Home Rule Bill defeated in House of Lords.

1894

5 March: Earl of Rosebery (Liberal) appointed Prime Minister.

1895

25 June: Salisbury appointed Prime Minister for third time.

July: General election – in Ireland, 69 Irish Party, 17 Unionist, 12 Parnellite,
     four Liberal Unionist, and one Liberal candidates returned to parlia-
     ment.

16 July: McCarthy re-elected for North Longford.

13 November: Healy et al. expelled from executive of Irish National
     Federation.

1896

1 February: McCarthy's resignation as chairman of Irish Party announced.

18 February: Dillon elected chairman of Irish Party, with McCarthy's
     support.

1897

c. April: McCarthy suffers physical breakdown.

1899

7 February: Dillon resigns as chairman of Irish Party.

1900

6 February: Redmond elected chairman of reunited Irish Party.

25 September: Dissolution of parliament; McCarthy retires from politics.

1901

22 January: Death of Queen Victoria; accession of King Edward VII.

1902

12 July: Arthur Balfour (Conservative) appointed Prime Minister.

October: Balfour recommends McCarthy for a Civil List pension, for
     services to literature.

1904

McCarthy's *The Story of an Irishman* published.

1905

5 December: Sir Henry Campbell-Bannerman (Liberal) appointed Prime Minister.

1908

8 April: Herbert Henry Asquith (Liberal) appointed Prime Minister.

1910

21 February: Sir Edward Carson becomes leader of Irish Unionist Parliamentary Party.

6 May: Death of King Edward VII; accession of King George V.

1911

18 August: Parliament Act limits powers of House of Lords.

McCarthy's last book, *Irish Recollections*, published.

1912

11 April: Third Home Rule Bill introduced into House of Commons.

24 April: Death of Justin McCarthy (Folkestone).

1936

20 March: Death of Justin Huntly McCarthy.

1943

4 November: Death of Charlotte Ely McCarthy.

Introduction

This is the second edition of a biography of Justin McCarthy (1830–1912).

McCarthy was, in sequence – and often at the same time – a journalist, essayist, newspaper editor, novelist, lecturer, and historian. He was also an MP. In the latter position, he was leader of the Irish Parliamentary Party during the crucial period from December 1890 until February 1896.[1]

Before his election as chairman (following the Parnell divorce controversy and the split in the Irish Party), McCarthy had been party vice-chairman since 1880. Despite his long tenure of these important positions, he remains largely forgotten, and his role in the struggle for Irish Home Rule is not adequately acknowledged. Why is this so?

Born in Cork in 1830, McCarthy moved to England in 1853, where he lived until his death in 1912. He played only a minor role in the much publicised land agitation of the 1880s, and consequently never built up a high profile in Ireland. Choosing instead to make his living as a journalist and author in London, he campaigned in England on behalf of Irish Home Rule, and attained a respected position in British political circles. As party chairman in the 1890s, he continued to concentrate his efforts in England, working especially for the maintenance of the alliance with the Liberal Party, while his colleagues focused on developments in Ireland.

McCarthy, therefore, despite his long and crucial role in the history of the Irish Party, never developed a lasting reputation in Ireland. Coming shortly after his death, the 1916 Easter Rising changed the direction of Irish nationalism and, in those stirring, militant times, the London-based Irish nationalist who had sought to reach a political compromise with Britain was quickly forgotten.

McCarthy's place in history rests on two related, but distinct, achievements. The first concerns his pivotal role in the mainten-ance of the unity of the Irish Party in the years of his chairmanship. During this turbulent period, the Irish Party fought a bruising and bitter political civil war against the breakaway Parnellites. The party was also involved in potentially more-damaging, long-running internal feuds, which threatened further to divide it. Through his conciliatory political approach, McCarthy ensured that the Irish Party did not once more split into separate factions.

McCarthy's second major achievement relates to his involvement in the passage, by the House of Commons, of the 1893 Home Rule Bill. By maintaining the unity of the Irish Party, he was also able to ensure that Home Rule remained at the top of the Westminster agenda. If the Irish Party had further split in 1892 or 1893, the second Home Rule Bill would not have been introduced into parlia-ment. By keeping the party unified, he saw the 1893 Home Rule Bill passed by the Commons. He thus succeeded where his predecessor, Charles Stewart Parnell, had failed, and he consequently helped to maintain constitutional politics in Ireland.

As a consequence of his successful career as a London journalist and editor, McCarthy was on friendly terms with leading British Radicals and Liberals, from the 1860s to the end of his political career. His novels and histories were critical and popular successes. According to one commentator, 'Had he been nothing but a writer, he would certainly have died rich, for his novels had real charm.'[2] McCarthy chose instead to devote himself to the Home Rule struggle and, as a result, in retirement required a British Civil List literary pension to keep him in reasonable comfort. The fact that the pension was recommended by a Conservative Prime Minister illustrates the high regard in which he was held, even by his political rivals.

CHAPTER I

The Making of an Irish Nationalist, 1830–53

George IV, King of Great Britain and Ireland, died in June 1830 and was succeeded by his brother, William IV. Following William's accession, the obligatory general election took place later that summer. The Tory Duke of Wellington subsequently suffered an unexpected defeat in parliament, and was replaced as Prime Minister by the Whig Earl Grey on 22 November 1830. The same day, Justin McCarthy was born near Cork city.

McCarthy was born and died (1912) in decades of momentous political developments. The 1830s saw Daniel O'Connell establish his first Repeal organisation, the passing of the Great Reform Act, and the tithe war. The 1910s witnessed the passing of the third Home Rule Bill, the First World War, and the Easter Rising.

Although McCarthy's historical importance stems from his political activities, his early interests were mostly literary. The McCarthys were an educated and artistic family. Justin's mother, the former Ellen Fitzgerald Canty, was reportedly distantly related to the German philosopher, Immanuel Kant. McCarthy's father, Michael Francis, had hoped to become a barrister but was for financial reasons unable to pursue that career. He rose instead to become chief clerk to the Cork city magistrates, and devoted his spare time to literary pursuits. McCarthy's elder sister, Ely, had her poems and her translations from French and Italian published locally; while his younger brother, Frank, went on to have his paintings hung in art galleries.

McCarthy's own education had a literary bent. At school he learned to read Latin and Greek fluently, and around this time he also acquired a knowledge of French, German, and Italian. Extra-curricular activities also helped to form the young scholar. He enrolled in the local Temperance Institute, the well-stocked library, lecture theatre and debating chamber of which provided early training for the future author and parliamentarian. In its library McCarthy first saw the periodical issues of Dickens's *Pickwick Papers*, and the Institute's programme for 1845–6 included McCarthy's lecture, 'On the Progress of the Drama'.[1]

National issues soon caught McCarthy's attention. Frustrated with the old Cork Scientific and Literary Society, and the 'non-political character and steady loyalty of its opinions', McCarthy and other young men seem to have come under the influence of the romantic nationalism of the *Nation* newspaper, and later formed the Cork Historical Society, in which they could 'give some expression to our patriotic impulses and yearnings'.[2]

McCarthy left school around the age of fifteen and joined a solicitor's firm. He had, he later wrote, been brought up in what 'might well have been described . . . [as] "genteel poverty"'.[3] It has been suggested, however, that his circumstances 'grew in poverty and lost in gentility as his easy-going dilettante father . . . came down in the world'.[4] Whether due to the actions of his father, or as a result of other factors, there was a sudden decline in the family fortune. The young McCarthy was forced to end his legal studies after about a year, and he managed to find paid employment with a family friend, John Francis Maguire. Maguire had founded the *Cork Examiner* in August 1841, as a liberal paper that support-ed Daniel O'Connell in his opposition to the Protestant and conservative *Cork Constitution*. McCarthy's nationalist impulses were strengthened by his early experiences as a journalist with the *Examiner* when, as a roving 'special correspondent' during the famine winter of 1846–7, he 'grew terribly familiar . . . with the frequent sight of death in some of its most heart-rending shapes'.[5] In the offices of the *Examiner* he came into contact with leading Young Irelanders, among them Thomas Francis Meagher and John Mitchel. A combination of these experiences strengthened the nationalist leanings of the young journalist, as did his presence (as one of the *Examiner*'s reporters) at the 1848 high treason trials of MP William Smith O'Brien, Thomas Francis Meagher, and their co-accused. At these trials McCarthy saw defence advocate Isaac Butt 'pour forth his magnificent declamation before the judges and the jury in the Court House at Clonmel'.[6]

Some two years later McCarthy once more encountered barrister Butt, this time in the Court House in Tralee, in a case of more local rather than national significance. McCarthy was again reporting for the *Examiner*, and the case concerned the alleged theft of cash by a 'young and rather pretty' post-mistress.[7] The chief witness for the prosecution was none other than Anthony Trollope, who had yet to publish his Barchester novels, and was then employed as a deputy post-office surveyor. McCarthy was later to know both the barrister and the witness – the former, when a famous politician, the latter, when a successful novelist.

In the period between these two cases, in the aftermath of the failed Young Ireland rebellion, McCarthy decided to join the '1849 movement', a secret conspiracy organised by youthful veterans of 1848. Grandiose plans, which included the proposed kidnapping of Queen Victoria during her visit to Dublin in August 1849, came to nought. The '1849 movement' soon collapsed, thereby ending McCarthy's 'only active personal share in the traditional work of

Irish rebellion against English rule'.[8] His subsequent nationalist activities would be purely constitutional.

McCarthy's remaining four years in Cork were chiefly devoted to earning sufficient income to support his family, while endeavouring to secure a position for himself in London journalism and the world of literature. There was for him no dichotomy between wanting to see a self-governing Ireland and making a living as a scribe in London. For an ambitious journalist in search of a literary career, Cork provided too limited a horizon.

McCarthy first went to London in February 1852. He visited galleries and attended the theatre, spending some time in both Houses of Parliament, the highlight of which was witnessing a brief speech in the Lords by the aged Duke of Wellington. The London visit did not prove successful in career terms and McCarthy returned to Cork, having failed to find new employment. He remained determined, however, to move from the Lee to the Thames.

In 1852 a commission was appointed to inquire into the existing state of fairs and markets in Ireland. When it reached Cork, the position of commission secretary unexpectedly became vacant and the commissioner, having read McCarthy's newspaper reports of its hearings, offered him the post. The main function of the secretary was to take shorthand notes of the daily proceedings of the inquiry, in preparation for a report to the government. McCarthy got leave of absence from the *Examiner* and joined the commission in early December 1852. He travelled throughout the country until February 1853 and was then temporarily based in Dublin, working on the report. It was to be his sole paid appointment under the crown.

The commission's work completed, McCarthy returned to the *Examiner* for a brief period. Over the years, his family situation had changed significantly. His sister, Ely, had died and his brother,

Frank, had availed of assisted passage to America. These departures meant a lessening of both his family responsibilities and his
ties with Cork. In 1853, having been offered a post with the newly
founded *Northern Daily Times* in Liverpool, McCarthy left his
native city and began his career with the English liberal press.

CHAPTER 2

The Development of a Liberal Propagandist, 1853–79

Between his arrival in Liverpool in 1853 and his entry into parliament in 1879, McCarthy progressed from provincial reporter to metropolitan leader-writer and successful author. He achieved considerable success as a journalist, editor, author, and lecturer. He used his pen and his voice consistently, both in Britain and in the United States, to support liberal causes and the extension of democratic reforms. He consequently became a well-known figure in liberal political and literary circles.

In its first issue, the *Northern Daily Times* proclaimed 'the Press . . . the guardian of the People's interests', and promised to support franchise reform and the general improvement of the condition of the masses.[1] McCarthy commenced work for the newspaper as a reporter, covering the courts and meetings of the Liverpool Town Council as well as general events. He quickly expanded his brief, however, and also became the paper's artistic, literary and dramatic critic. In time, he was to write some of its leading articles and was appointed to the editorial staff.

McCarthy saw the job of reporter as a stepping-stone to a career in literature. With this in mind, he gave public lectures on German authors such as Goethe and Schiller, and on the British novelists, Fielding and Smollett. He also contributed to the Methodist-linked *London Quarterly Review* – the first periodical in the capital to publish his articles.

Ambition had prompted McCarthy to move to Liverpool, and it is likely that the same ambition prompted him to make personal contact with William Ewart Gladstone who, in Chester in November 1855, delivered a lecture on the colonies. Gladstone had earlier in the year resigned as Chancellor of the Exchequer, and considered the lecture 'much below what it should have been',[2] but McCarthy requested permission to publish it in pamphlet form.[3] He assured Gladstone that it was not unusual 'in London or in the provinces to republish in this manner any remarkable lecture or address of a distinguished statesman, calculated to command more than mere passing interest given to the contents of a newspaper'.[4] The flattery worked, and permission to publish was granted.

Earlier that year, on 27 March 1855, McCarthy had married Charlotte Allman, whom he had first met in February 1852, when he was staying with her brother in Liverpool en route to London.[5] Charlotte's father, William George Allman, was from Bandon, County Cork. Although McCarthy was raised as a Roman Catholic, he and Charlotte were married in the Presbyterian King Edward Street Chapel in Macclesfield. They were to have two children, Justin Huntly, born 30 September 1856, and Charlotte Ely, born 7 July 1859.

McCarthy's writings attracted attention, and in January 1860 the family moved to London, where McCarthy had secured a job with the *Morning Star*. The *Star* preached the radical reform message of the Cobden–Bright Manchester School, which favoured free trade and international arbitration. John Bright, 'the most important figure in the history of mid-Victorian radicalism',[6] was a member of *Star*'s board of management. He regularly visited the newspaper's offices, and was a major influence on both the *Star* and McCarthy. While a reporter with the *Star*, McCarthy sent his essay on Voltaire's romances to the quarterly *Westminster Review*.[7] Immediate publication of this unsolicited essay was followed by a request from the *Westminster* for more material.

In London, McCarthy came into contact with most of the major literary figures of the day. He met Charles Dickens on many occasions, and considered him to be 'the very best after-dinner speaker I ever heard'.[8] He also admired William Makepeace Thackeray and, but for an accident of fate, the two might well have become friends.

Never overawed by Thackeray, as he was by Dickens, McCarthy had met Thackeray casually a number of times, before he (McCarthy) wrote an anonymous piece in the *Morning Star* that caught Thackeray's attention. The latter established that McCarthy was the author of the piece, and invited him to 'a small dinner-party confined to a few literary men' over Christmas 1863. McCarthy was delighted with the invitation, commenting later that

> No favour that any sovereign could bestow upon me, had any sovereign been in the least likely to single me out for any mark of favour, could have filled me with such rapture as I received from that token of Thackeray's goodwill. I am afraid that for some days after I made myself rather a nuisance to my friends and acquaintances by my announcement, apparently in quite a casual sort of way, that I had been invited to dine at Thackeray's house.[9]

A few days before the anticipated dinner, McCarthy learned of Thackeray's unexpected death, following a stroke. He later admitted that his initial reaction was to 'think for the time more of my own personal loss than of the loss which the world of letters had sustained'.[10] Instead of a Christmas-season dinner and a possible friendship, McCarthy had to be satisfied with subsequently purchasing a volume by Smollett, once owned by Thackeray, upon which the latter had written notes in the margin.

Around this time, McCarthy began to make his own name as a novelist. While his formal employment continued with the *Star*,

he also found time to write *Paul Massie* (1866), a novel 'all
throbbing with sensation',[11] *The Waterdale Neighbours* (1867), and
My Enemy's Daughter (1869).

By January 1861 McCarthy had become the *Star*'s foreign
editor. His chief qualification for the post was, he believed, his
ability to read and translate French, German, Italian and Spanish
newspapers. While foreign editor, his sole expedition abroad as a
special correspondent brought him first to Königsberg, and then
to Berlin, for the coronation of King William I of Prussia in
October 1861. During this visit McCarthy had the pleasure of
meeting the newly self-crowned king – the only monarch to whom
he was ever presented. The trip was made all the more memorable
by two meetings with a 'genial Herr von Bismarck', then Prussian
ambassador in St Petersburg.

Bismarck, never shy about self-promotion, asked to meet some
of the English journalists who were covering the coronation. In
advance of their first meeting, McCarthy prepared a short speech
in German, and was somewhat nervous as he was approached by a
'gigantic figure, in the steel corselet and white uniform of his
cuirassier regiment'.[12] (Bismarck later wrote to his sister that he
had worn the uniform and a wig in order to keep himself warm
during the two-hour, outdoor coronation ceremony.[13])

When they met, Bismarck put McCarthy immediately at ease by
saying, in fluent and idiomatic (though heavily accented) English,
that he was more than happy to talk in the latter's native tongue,
good-humouredly adding that he 'could exchange London chaff
with a London cabman'.[14] Bismarck proved to be well informed
about English journalism, and had a wide knowledge of English
literature.

During the early 1860s, however, foreign affairs were dominated
not by European but by North American events. Bright, the
Morning Star, and McCarthy (whose brother fought on the Union

side) took a major interest in the American Civil War, and supported a strong pro–Northern stance. In London, the government
and the bulk of the press championed the Southern cause, but
Bright made much of the view that England was made up of two
nations: one, the governing aristocracy who supported the South;
and the other, the labouring masses who supported the North. In
later years McCarthy was to adapt this message to the Irish situation, when he sought to gain the backing of the labouring masses
for another cause of freedom – that of Home Rule for Ireland.

Despite being away from Ireland, and his immersion in radical
British politics, McCarthy never lost his interest in Irish affairs. He
had kept in touch with Irish colleagues such as his school-friend,
Tom Crosbie, with whom he corresponded on personal and political
matters. (Crosbie edited the *Cork Examiner* while John Francis
Maguire was in London on political business, and bought the
newspaper in 1873, following Maguire's death the previous year.)
McCarthy also maintained contact with his one-time employer,
Maguire, a long-time MP, and became acquainted with the former
Young Ireland fugitive, John Blake Dillon. Dillon was elected an
MP in 1865, only to die the following year aged 52, from cholera
contracted in Dublin.[15] McCarthy also wrote regularly for the *Star*
on Irish matters, the most contentious of which during the 1860s
was Fenianism.

McCarthy's diary for 1867[16] reveals his interest in, and his
sympathy for, the Irish rebels. On 12 February 1867 he wrote, 'Great
Fenian attack on Chester Castle!' and on 6 March, 'Told her
[Charlotte] of great Fenian uprising in Ireland.' He even hoped for
some success. On 12 March he wrote, 'Fenians still disturbing the
government – thank goodness'. It was, however, not his diary entries
but his public writings in late 1867 that were to lead to criticism.

McCarthy had been appointed editor of the *Star* in 1865 and so
he directed that paper's response to Fenian activities in both

Ireland and Britain. On 23 November 1867 three Fenians (William Philip Allen, Michael Larkin, and Michael O'Brien) were executed at Salford, having been found guilty of the murder of a Manchester police officer, Sergeant Brett, during the rescue of two Fenian prisoners the previous September. The execution of the 'Manchester Martyrs' inflamed passions on both sides of the Irish Sea, and on 26 November McCarthy recorded in his diary that his 'Office got lots of letters about my article on Ireland'. On 13 December an explosion beside Clerkenwell jail in London, intended to facilitate the escape of Fenian prisoners, caused multiple deaths and injuries to local residents. A predictable anti-Irish backlash followed. The *Morning Star* office, McCarthy wrote, 'got heaps of abusive letters accusing me of Fenianism'.[17] Passions would eventually subside, but McCarthy had shown, by what he had published in the *Star*, that he was prepared to sacrifice his popularity and speak out in defence of his fellow-countrymen.

Somewhat ironically, in view of all the criticism McCarthy received for supporting the Fenians, he and the *Morning Star* occasionally came in for criticism 'for not pleading the case of the Fenians as often and as earnestly' as one English critic thought they should.[18] That critic was John Bright.

Bright had, for a few years before the Fenian rising, been endeavouring to gain the support of Irish popular interests for Gladstone and liberal reforms. At the 1865 general election in Ireland – before the advent of the Home Rule movement – the Liberals had won 58 seats, the Conservatives, 47. In November 1866 Bright had visited Ireland, and was proclaimed 'the first Englishman to make himself thoroughly popular in Ireland'. His trip was a considerable success, as 'Nobody had commanded this range of support in Ireland since O'Connell's day.'[19]

Bright now brushed aside McCarthy's concerns about his obligations, as editor, to consider the 'interests of the paper and its proprietors', in the face of growing unpopularity among the British public. Bright uncompromisingly argued that the interests of the proprietors came second to 'what was right and just', while McCarthy, not unreasonably, 'argued that if we pressed the matter too far, we should only cease to have any hearing at all from the British public'.[20] Whatever about the merits of Bright's view regarding the ignoring of the proprietors' interests, he was surely right when he wrote to McCarthy in early November 1867 that to hang 'the Manchester Fenians . . . will embitter the whole Irish question'.[21]

McCarthy resigned from the *Star* in June 1868, and took his family to America the following September. He claimed that his main reason for leaving the newspaper was the anticipated departure of Bright from its board (to join a future Liberal government), although financial considerations probably also influenced his decision. The *Star* was not commercially successful – sales were falling, it was losing money, and McCarthy's pay was consequently low. While London editors were then averaging close to £1,000 per annum, the editor of the *Star* was receiving only ten guineas a week in the 1860s.[22] When, in February 1868, a change of ownership was mooted, McCarthy decided to resign. (The *Star* finally ceased publication in late 1869, its last editor being John Morley).

There were also personal reasons for McCarthy's decision to resign. In 1861 his mother, Ellen, had come to London and had lived with the McCarthy family until her death in 1865. For some unexplained reason, his father, Michael Francis, had remained in Cork, where he died in 1864. It would appear that the father–son relationship was not particularly close. Diary entries such as 'Letter from Tom Crosbie about *him*',[23] and 'letter from Tom Crosbie . . . announcing the death of M.F.McC.'[24] confirm this view. With both parents dead, McCarthy now decided to visit his brother Frank in America.

Prominent Americans whom he had known in London, because of the *Star*'s support for the Union side in the Civil War, were

among those who now provided McCarthy with letters of introduction. In America he took up an editorial position with the New
York *Independent* (like the *Star*, a pro-reform newspaper), writing
on various subjects of English and wider European concern. His
position brought him into contact with many political leaders on
the Union side of the recent conflict. He also met Union military
leaders, including General George Armstrong Custer, 'the dashing
cavalry officer . . . with an abundance of thick yellow hair'.[25]

McCarthy was also welcomed into the literary circles of New
York and Boston, where he met and befriended writers such as
James Russell Lowell, Ralph Waldo Emerson, and Henry Wads-
worth Longfellow. In addition to his work for the *Independent*,
McCarthy wrote leading articles for the New York *Tribune*, and
while in New York he was contracted to supply *Harper's Monthly*
with short stories. This contract, and a long-running agreement
with the *Galaxy*, a New York literary magazine, allowed him the
freedom to indulge his wish to travel. From cities as far apart as San
Francisco, Minneapolis, and New Orleans, he sent his contributions back to New York. During the period 1868 to 1871, he
reportedly visited 35 of the then 37 United States.

The McCarthy family came back to England in May 1870, but
returned to America in time for McCarthy to undertake a lecture
tour, which ran from November 1870 to February 1871. Poor sight
prevented him from reading his lectures, but he had already developed the practice of preparing his ideas in advance, and trusting
'to the moment of speaking for the form of words my thoughts
were to adopt'.[26] His lecture topics ranged from new publications
to notable public figures and contemporary issues, and the tour
appears to have been a financial, critical, and personal success. In
December 1870, having commented favourably on McCarthy's
'able and scholarly address' on the Franco-Prussian War, the Fort
Wayne *Sentinel* went on to describe the speaker as

a man of medium height, rather heavy set, of a florid complexion, long flowing hair brushed neatly back from his forehead, and appears to advantage as a lecturer. His manner is smooth, easy, graceful and dignified, speaking in a rich, mellow voice, without hesitation.[27]

While McCarthy was receiving such public praise his wife, Charlotte, was suffering privately from depression, and was drinking excessively.[28]

McCarthy settled easily into life in America. His brother, Frank, lived with his family in New Jersey, and McCarthy also had his professional activities and colleagues for stimulation and company. Charlotte had no such outlets and was unable to adjust to life in America. She and the children remained in New York when McCarthy started his lecture tour in mid-November 1870. By mid-January 1871 she was writing in her diary, 'Wish I had staid in Europe where I have some friends.'[29] In early February she recorded that she was 'home sick & heart sick'.[30] Faced with these domestic circumstances, McCarthy, who had hoped to make more money for less effort in America than would be possible in England, decided to return to London. Although he was careful in later life to claim publicly that his decision to leave America had been prompted by a desire to help the cause of Irish nationalism, he did reveal that his wife's unhappiness was the main motive for his decision to return to England.

The family arrived back in England in June 1871, and McCarthy settled down in the capital to the life of a journalist and author. He had begun writing for the liberal *Daily News* (until 1895 an 'unwaveringly Gladstonian'[31] publication) when he had visited London in mid-1870, and he returned to that newspaper as a parliamentary leader writer in 1871. As a writer for the *Daily News*, he had easy access to many London functions, which he often attended with Charlotte. T. P. O'Connor, McCarthy's soon-to-be parliamentary colleague, later described the couple as 'indefatigable theatre-goers . . . [who] were never apart', and went on to say that Charlotte, with 'a vast mass of white hair drawn back from her forehead . . . excited attention'.[32]

As a leader writer rather than an editor, McCarthy had more time to devote to other writing. In addition to his political output and occasional literary articles for the *News*, he contributed to various periodicals on both sides of the Atlantic. His higher profile in the 1870s was, however, established predominantly on the basis of his novels. These included *A Fair Saxon* (1873), *Dear Lady Distain* (1875), and *Miss Misanthrope* (1878). Due to the high cost of novels at that time, authors were largely dependent on libraries, such as Mudie's, purchasing their works.[33] According to O'Connor, McCarthy believed 'that a novelist should have in his mind's eye in all his stories the unmarried girl of seventeen or eighteen; they were the main body of novel readers', and that libraries consequently targeted their marketing at this group. O'Connor estimated that, in the late 1870s, McCarthy 'must have been earning . . . the gigantic income of two or three thousand a year'.[34] Additional professional renown, and income, came from the publication of his non-fiction works.

In late 1878 the first two volumes of McCarthy's *A History of Our Own Times* were published. These dealt with the politics and literature of the period, from the accession of Queen Victoria in 1837 to the end of the Crimean War in 1856. Five additional volumes would later be published, bringing the history up to 1901 and the accession of King Edward VII. Several reprints, new editions, abridgements, and translations testify to the success and popularity of the work. It was estimated that the *History* had by the 1880s brought McCarthy a profit of £6,000. Shortly after the publication of the first two volumes, he embarked on his own political career.

Gladstone, while Prime Minister from 1868 to 1874, had introduced major legislative reforms for Ireland (such as the disestablishment of the Church of Ireland), which had gained him considerable support among the Irish Roman Catholic population. These reforms were not universally popular in Ireland and, ironically, helped to give birth to the Home Rule movement. At a meeting in May 1870 convened by Isaac Butt (the son of an Anglican clergyman), disparate but mutually disgruntled elements had come together and unanimously adopted a resolution calling for 'the establishment of an Irish parliament with full control over our own domestic affairs'.[35] The resultant Home Government Association was a conservative and narrowly based movement but, by 1873, with the establishment of the Home Rule League, more radical elements, including a number of Fenians, had widened its appeal and altered its direction.

McCarthy's early involvement in the Home Rule movement is still somewhat unclear, but it is known that, after a visit to Ireland in early 1872, he wrote for the *Daily News* on the subject, and that in April 1873 he spoke at a Home Rule meeting in London. He was also in private contact with Home Rule MPs, and his links with the movement must have been considered close, as the *Pall Mall Gazette* announced in January 1874 that he would be the movement's candidate for the constituency of Bandon at the forthcoming general election. Although this was untrue, it was the first time McCarthy had been publicly mentioned as a possible parliamentary candidate.

The 1874 general election was the first to be held since the founding of the Home Government Association, and resulted in the return of 59 Home Rulers to parliament. This group did not constitute a united party, and included members of both moderate and more-advanced nationalist views. The latter constituted a minority of the Home Rulers, but from 1875 drew attention to themselves in the House of Commons. They did so by exploiting parliamentary procedures in order deliberately to obstruct Commons business, by making lengthy speeches on non-Irish issues.

McCarthy was able to maintain links with both sides of the party. From at least the early 1870s he and Charlotte were in contact with the moderate William Shaw, MP, a Cork merchant and banker, who was apparently related to Charlotte's family. In addition, McCarthy's social and political circles soon included a young Wicklow landlord – Charles Stewart Parnell.

Parnell was first elected to parliament in 1875. He and McCarthy met the following year and, being near neighbours in London, they frequently travelled together to the Commons, with the former heading for the debating chamber, the latter for the reporters' gallery. Despite Parnell's almost total lack of interest in literature – McCarthy considered that for Parnell 'all the great poets and prose writers had lived in vain, so far as he was concerned'[36] – the two formed a close friendship. Parnell was particularly popular with the McCarthy children, owing to 'his sympathetic ways and the genial ease with which he made himself interested in their occupations', and McCarthy concluded that he had 'never met . . . a better-bred man than Parnell'.[37]

With contacts at the highest levels on both the moderate and obstructionist sides of the Home Rule party, McCarthy was appointed in March 1877 to the council of the Home Rule movement in London. This position brought him to the heart of the Home Rule power structure, and renewed his acquaintance with the party's leader, Isaac Butt, whom he had known in the 1860s when he (McCarthy) was editor of the *Morning Star*. At that time, Butt used to visit its newspaper office to discuss Irish affairs, as the *Star* 'was always in favour of fair play to Ireland'.[38] During the trials of some Fenians in Ireland, Butt had objected to what he considered certain irregularities on the part of the Crown in the conduct of those proceedings, and had wanted to bring these alleged irregularities before the English public. Butt contended that these would never have been tolerated in an English court of criminal law, and McCarthy had used his discretion as editor to publish an anonymous letter from Butt in the *Star*, objecting to the Crown's *modus operandi*. McCarthy was subsequently amused when a Tory newspaper, commenting on the *Star*'s anonymous letter, declared that the writer must be as ignorant of Irish, as he was of English, courts. McCarthy's amusement stemmed from the fact that Butt was then one of the leading advocates at the Irish Bar.

Moving in such political circles, and with a 'very decided taste for politics and political subjects',[39] McCarthy later wrote that he felt 'little doubt . . . that whenever a vacancy occurred in one or other of certain Irish constituencies I should be invited to offer myself as a candidate for the vacant seat'.[40]

T. P. O'Connor later recalled, with perhaps some friendly exaggeration, that McCarthy was, in the late 1870s, 'a man of fascinatingly agreeable manners, gentle, modest, as brilliant in talk as in writing, [who] was the darling of London society'. Without exaggeration, however, O'Connor continued that McCarthy 'would have been an acceptable candidate for the Liberal Party . . . [as] in the main he was in thorough agreement with them'.[41]

It is true that McCarthy's London career since 1860 could have in many ways prepared him for membership of the House under the Liberal standard. He had contact with Gladstone, was friendly with Bright, and possessed a written and verbal fluency that would have made him an asset to any political party. While ambitious to become a member of the House, McCarthy chose to align that ambition with patriotism. Major Myles O'Reilly, a Home Rule MP who had topped the poll in the Longford County constituency in the 1874 general election, resigned his position in 1879 when he was appointed as an assistant commissioner of intermediate

education.[42] In March of that year McCarthy accepted an invitation to contest the resultant vacancy for the County of Longford,
as the Home Rule candidate.

At home one evening, and just about to operate as unofficial
stage-manager for a youthful domestic production of *Love's
Labour's Lost*, McCarthy received a telegram requesting him to
come immediately to Longford, and offer himself as a candidate.
He crossed to Ireland 'as soon as the train bound for Holyhead
could convey [him]', thereby exchanging what he termed 'private
theatricals in our Fitzroy Square Bohemia'[43] for the world's
greatest public theatre – the Palace of Westminster.

Longford County was a nationalist stronghold, and McCarthy
had only to secure the nomination of the local nationalists in order
to guarantee his election. Addressing the voters of that constituency for the first time, he declared that, if elected, he

> would be found in the ranks of the Irish Party in Parliament, working
> cordially on the great question of Home Rule, Catholic Education,
> Fixity of Tenure, Reform of the Grand Jury Laws, and the
> Equalisation of the Franchise.[44]

McCarthy appeared before a meeting of the Roman Catholic
clergy of Longford on 27 March and secured the almost-essential
clerical recommendation to the electors. Four days later, a meeting
of the priests and people of the county selected him as their
candidate for the forthcoming election, with McCarthy 'expressing
his thorough concurrence in the programme of the clergy'.[45] On 4
April 1879, no rival candidate having being proposed, he was
declared duly elected member of parliament for the County of
Longford.[46] He was 48.

CHAPTER 3

Vice-Chairman, 1880–90

McCarthy's election to parliament in April 1879 was quickly followed by the death of the Home Rule Party leader, Isaac Butt, on 5 May. William Shaw was elected sessional chairman of the party in Butt's place. Later that summer, personal tragedy was to follow for McCarthy. On 15 August 1879 – her 48th birthday – Charlotte McCarthy died of cirrhosis of the liver. She had been unwell for some years.

The party into which McCarthy was first elected in 1879, and to which he was re-elected in 1880,[1] was not a monolithic organisation. Rival factions gathered around the moderate leader, Shaw, and the obstructionist, Parnell. In the general election of April 1880, 61 nominal Home Rulers were returned to parliament and, when the party met in Dublin on 17 May, Parnell narrowly defeated Shaw by 23 votes to 18 for the position of sessional chairman. The overwhelming majority of Parnell's supporters, who included McCarthy, were recently elected MPs.

In his speech supporting Parnell before the leadership vote, McCarthy displayed his conciliatory approach, claiming to be 'qualified to speak impartially' on the question of whether Shaw or Parnell should be elected chairman, because he professed 'a friendship with both gentlemen which is not limited to acquaintanceship in the House of Commons, but extends outside it'. McCarthy urged Shaw to avoid a division and to step aside in favour of

Parnell. The results of the recent general election, McCarthy
said, had clearly shown that Parnell was the people's choice, and
McCarthy declared himself consequently in favour of making
Parnell 'the leader of the Irish party in Parliament'.[2]

In 1880 Gladstone became Prime Minister for the second time.
This was McCarthy's first experience of a Liberal government,
and the change of administration presented him with a dilemma.
As 'a Radical, so far as English politics were concerned',[3] it was
natural that he would oppose Disraeli's outgoing Conservative
government. In 1872 he had written that

> An average Tory really is a stupid man . . . His mind is narrow, dull,
> inflexible; he cannot connect cause with effect, or see that a change is
> coming, or why it should come . . .You cannot help liking him, and
> sometimes laughing at him.[4]

Opposition to a Liberal government led by Gladstone was a very
different matter.

McCarthy was generally an enthusiastic supporter of liberal
causes and reforms, and was an admirer – and subsequently
biographer[5] – of Gladstone. He therefore found the period of
obstructionist opposition, from the introduction of coercion
legislation in 1881 to the Kilmainham 'Treaty' of 1882, an un-
pleasant experience. To appreciate the personal sacrifice that
McCarthy had to make to support the obstructionist policy, it is
necessary to consider his position in English society, and especially
his attitude to Gladstone.

After their initial contact in 1855, it would be twelve years
before McCarthy and Gladstone were to communicate again. In
February 1867 Gladstone took exception to an article in the *Morning
Star* and complained about it to the newspaper's editor, McCarthy.
In reply, McCarthy issued a fulsome apology, and availed of the

opportunity to remind the Liberal leader of their former Liverpool connection, and of the 'courteous & friendly permission and assistance' that he (McCarthy) had previously received.[6] The following year, he found an opportunity to renew the correspondence.

In November 1868 McCarthy wrote an interesting letter to Gladstone (who was about to become Prime Minister for the first time) from New York.[7] Presuming on 'a very slight, impersonal sort of acquaintanceship', he brought to Gladstone's attention 'a fact which may not be without importance as an argument in favor of your policy [of disestablishment] with regard to the Irish Church'. McCarthy had, he said, recently met John Mitchel, the Young Ireland exile, whom he described as 'the bitterest enemy of English Rule in Ireland'. According to McCarthy, Mitchel was 'a man of remarkable ability' who 'insisted that [Gladstone] and John Bright are the worst and most dangerous enemies Ireland ever had – *because* you intend to abolish grievances and injustices', such as the established position of the Church of Ireland. Mitchel feared that the removal of such grievances would lead to a reconciliation between Ireland and England. Unlike Mitchel, who advocated a policy of armed insurrection and separation, McCarthy supported Gladstone and a dual policy of justice and reconciliation.[8] McCarthy does not appear to have been in contact again with Gladstone until January 1879, when he had his publisher send Gladstone the first two volumes of his *A History of Our Own Times*, 'as the only tribute of admiration and respect which it is in my power to offer to you'.[9]

Despite his lack of direct contact with the Liberal leader during the 1870s, this was a period during which McCarthy became increasingly involved in liberal clubs and social life. In mid-1870 he was elected a member of the Cobden Club, which introduced him to some of the current and future leaders of liberal politics in England. The club's 1873 membership list included 180 members of parliament (among them Prime Minister Gladstone) and two

future Liberal Prime Ministers, Lord Rosebery and Henry
Campbell-Bannerman. McCarthy also became a member of the
Royal Colonial Institute. When he was elected to this non-partisan
association in June 1874, its members included a former Liberal
Colonial and Foreign Secretary, Earl Granville, and the current
Conservative Colonial Secretary, the Earl of Carnarvon (a future
Irish viceroy).

McCarthy's acceptance into society was further emphasised by
his regular visits to notable London houses. In his memoirs he
fondly recalled hostesses such as Mrs Stanley (later Lady Jeune),
the Dowager Countess Russell (widow of Lord John Russell, who
had been Prime Minister during the Famine), and Lady Stanley of
Alderley, all of whom welcomed him into their homes. At Mrs
Stanley's house he dined with Sir Stafford Northcote, Conservative Chancellor of the Exchequer, and first met Lord Randolph
Churchill and Arthur Balfour. His social world therefore included
both Liberal and Conservative politicians of the first rank, years
before he became an MP. He was consequently risking his social, as
well as his financial, position when he supported the Irish Party's
obstruction campaign against the Gladstone government in
1881–2. William O'Brien, a fellow journalist and MP, later wrote
of McCarthy that 'No Irishman of our times made heavier
sacrifices'.[10] One social consequence arising from his involvement
in the obstructionist campaign was the ending of his friendship
with Lady Stanley.

The financial price was also significant for an author 'who had
been doing [his] best to win for [himself] a position in English
literature and journalism'.[11] In his autobiography, McCarthy
referred to his loss of popularity due to his political activities in the
early 1880s. He recalled that, 'During these troublesome times of
obstruction I found that the intense feeling aroused among the
general English public against the Irish obstructionists had a direct

effect on the sale of my books.'[12] Unlike Parnell, who often displayed antipathy towards the English and had his estate in Ireland, McCarthy lived in London, respected the English, admired their achievements, and was largely dependent upon them for his livelihood. Nevertheless, he supported the policy of obstruction, despite the personal cost involved. As he was fond of saying, 'A man must fight under his own flag.'[13]

These 'troublesome times of obstruction', as McCarthy called them, revolved around the issues of coercion and land reform. In 1879 a land war broke out in Ireland. Agricultural depression, successive poor harvests, evictions, and rising expectations led to a mood of unrest, which was capitalised upon by the exceptional leadership of Parnell and of the ticket-of-leave Fenian, Michael Davitt. When the new parliament first assembled in April 1880, Parnell's supporters, who constituted the more advanced wing of the party, were dismayed by the absence from the Queen's Speech of any reference to the land situation in Ireland, and they brought forward an amendment that drew attention to the crisis.

Speaking in favour of the amendment, McCarthy adopted a friendly rather than an obstructionist tone. He took care to emphasise his liberal sympathies, and told Gladstone – 'the great statesman now at the head of the Government' – that he 'rose in no spirit of hostility to Her Majesty's Government'. The land question was, he argued, 'the one great question before all others occupying the attention of the people of Ireland' and, although he did not expect a comprehensive solution in the short term, he called for a temporary measure, to check 'some of the worst evils of the existing land system', before long-term reforms were introduced.

McCarthy went on to say that the absence of any mention of the land question in the Queen's Speech had led to great disappointment in Ireland and (perhaps referring to his personal position) meant that the Irish people 'to an extent . . . felt distrust even of

their own Members who appeared to be too closely allied with the
Liberal Party'. Recalling the dictum that 'Ireland should be governed
in accordance with Irish ideas', he pointed out that 'the more that
idea was carried out, the more loyal would be the people of Ireland
to the Queen of the United Kingdom'.[14]

By the time parliament was prorogued on 7 September 1880,
land legislation had still to be passed, and the struggle for land
reform now transferred to Ireland. McCarthy was obliged to remain
in London to earn his living, while parliamentary colleagues such
as Parnell and John Dillon addressed protest meetings in Ireland.
These meetings had the dual effect of sharply reducing evictions
and leading to the prosecution of Land League leaders, including
Parnell, who were charged with conspiracy to prevent the payment
of rent.

On 27 December 1880, on the eve of the opening of the
conspiracy trial, McCarthy was elected to the newly created post
of vice-chairman of the party. In view of his impending trial, Parnell
considered it prudent to create this position, and he proposed
McCarthy for the job. The main reasons for McCarthy's election
appear to have been his seniority in the active wing of the party, his
standing as a respected journalist and author, and his personal
closeness to Parnell. His valuable contacts with English politicians
like his old friend, John Bright – 'still the doyen of the Left'[15] –
who was a member of Gladstone's new cabinet, and with Henry
Labouchere, the Radical MP for Northampton (who, as part-
proprietor of the *Daily News*, was McCarthy's employer), may
also have influenced his colleagues' selection of him as vice-
chairman. In modern parlance, a leadership team of Parnell, with
his mass following in Ireland, and McCarthy, with his connections
in English political circles, constituted the dream ticket.

In his acceptance speech McCarthy thanked his colleagues for
the honour of electing him to the new position, while expecting

'that the party will not have to depend very much on my leadership'. Under no circumstances, he said, should Parnell resign from his position, 'even if by any chance he should not be able to perform the full functions of the office'. If, however, Parnell were unable to attend parliament for a considerable time, McCarthy did 'not feel [himself] adequate to fulfil the functions of deputy-chairman, which would then become in fact those of chairman of the party'.[16] This lack of personal ambition was probably another factor in Parnell's choice of him as vice-chairman. Whether McCarthy's concerns were for personal or career reasons (the need to have adequate time to write and make a living), ten years later, when necessary, he would push them aside and reluctantly take on the often full-time role of party chairman.

In January 1881 Ireland was the main topic of the Queen's Speech, which promised both coercion and land reform. The Irish Party decried the former while calling for the latter, and for eleven nights its members strenuously obstructed and prolonged the debate on the speech. In mid-January 1881 William Shaw and eleven colleagues seceded from the Irish Party, having been effectively manoeuvred out by Parnell, who had begun 'to move cautiously towards the creation of that unified and disciplined parliamentary party which was to be his most striking political achievement'[17]. On 24 January the Irish Chief Secretary, William Edward Forster, introduced the promised coercion measure, the Protection of Person and Property (Ireland) Bill. This encountered prolonged obstruction – the sitting of 31 January lasted for over 41 hours and was brought to an end only by the Speaker putting the question on the morning of 2 February.

In the absence of Parnell, McCarthy led the opposition to the Speaker's *ultra vires* (at that time) action of ending the debate. Blocked in his subsequent attempts to open a new debate, McCarthy then led his colleagues out of the House. The Speaker's action in cutting short the debate marked the effective end of the campaign of obstruction. When, on 3 February, the Irish Party protested at the arrest of Michael Davitt, 36 Irish members, including McCarthy, were suspended from the Commons. New rules of procedure were adopted, obstruction was no longer a viable policy, and the coercive legislation was finally enacted on 2 March 1881.

With obstruction no longer an option, other methods of generating support for Ireland's cause, and for opposing coercion, had to be found. One of these was the National Land League of Great Britain. This organisation, established in London in late March 1881, sought to develop a communality between Irish tenant farmers and the British working classes – an idea very much in keeping with the aims of McCarthy, who became its first president.

As outlined in the Queen's Speech, coercion was followed by land reform, and in March 1881 Gladstone introduced a land bill. This established in law the long-desired 'three Fs' – fair rent, fixity of tenure, and free sale – and it was difficult for the party to mount an all-out attack on a measure that commanded considerable support, both in Ireland and within the Irish Party itself. Parnell indeed had difficulty in persuading the party to mount serious opposition to the government's proposals. At a party meeting on 5 May, he managed to win narrow support – by 18 votes to 11 – for his policy of abstention on its second reading, only after he had threatened to resign if he lost the vote. McCarthy was one of the eleven who voted against the abstention policy, which was an important early indication of his independence. Although Parnell's chosen deputy, he was prepared, when he considered it necessary, to vote against his leader. Having lost that vote, however, McCarthy refused to join the fourteen members of the now reduced party who disobeyed its decision, and who supported the bill at its second reading in the Commons.

Irish opinion was divided on the merits of the land bill but most, including the Roman Catholic hierarchy, welcomed it, and it became law on 22 August 1881. Parnell, although relatively moderate in his comments during the parliamentary session, adopted a more uncompromising tone on his return to Ireland. Following a series of public meetings and intemperate remarks, he was arrested on 13 October, under the coercion act. An unsuccessful 'no rent' manifesto was issued from jail on 18 October, and two days later the Land League was suppressed. Parnell was to remain in Kilmainham jail – except for a brief but crucial period of parole – until 2 May 1882.

McCarthy removed himself from the political arena in the autumn of 1881 when, with his son and daughter, he took an extended holiday in Europe, North Africa, and the Middle East. After a month in Athens (which would later result in his novel, *Maid of Athens*), he and his family visited Constantinople, Egypt, and the Holy Land. The leisurely return journey took in Cairo, Rome and Paris. He arrived back in London shortly after parliament reopened in February 1882.

The trip was presumably partly financed by the sale of McCarthy's *A History of Our Own Times*, the third and fourth volumes of which (continuing the story up to the general election of 1880) had been published in 1881. They achieved considerable critical success, with the *Observer* claiming that it had 'no hesitation in saying that it is one of the ablest works that the latter part of this century has produced'.[18] Back in London McCarthy found that he had limited time to devote to literary matters, as political developments were reaching a critical stage.

With Parnell still in Kilmainham, McCarthy was now the senior party figure in the Commons. In April the former used a temporary release from prison, due to the death of a nephew in Paris, to arrange a negotiated settlement. Prohibited from open political activity, he met McCarthy in London on the afternoon of his release. Three weeks of negotiations with the government followed – which would result in the Kilmainham 'Treaty'. McCarthy and Captain William O'Shea, the husband of Parnell's lover, Katharine, acted as the Irish negotiators. On 23 April Parnell had a lengthy meeting with McCarthy in London, before returning to Kilmainham the next day. On 25 April Parnell wrote to McCarthy, enclosing a memorandum of their conversation, which he suggested McCarthy show to Joseph Chamberlain, the President of the Board of Trade, who was known to have Irish sympathies. This McCarthy did, and Chamberlain undertook 'to make good use of it'.[19]

O'Shea undoubtedly played a more active role than McCarthy in the negotiations, but McCarthy, well known and respected in the Commons and also vice-chairman of the party, was the more credible negotiator. While O'Shea brought energy to the proceedings, McCarthy supplied the necessary gravitas. McCarthy was also in a good position to gauge the likely reaction of his fellow MPs to a compromise settlement. On 2 May Parnell and his fellow 'suspects' were released from Kilmainham jail.

In return for certain land reforms, in particular an arrears bill that brought tenants in arrears under the protection of the 1881 Land Act, Parnell was obliged by the Kilmainham 'Treaty' 'to co-operate cordially for the future with the Liberal Party in forwarding Liberal principles'.[20] Two events – the Phoenix Park murders (6 May 1882) of the newly appointed Chief Secretary, Lord Frederick Cavendish, and the Under-Secretary, Thomas Burke, and the concomitant Prevention of Crime Act – were, however, to delay the start of this period of cordial co-operation between the Irish Party and the Liberal government. The double murder threw the Irish Party into a state of crisis.

On 7 May McCarthy received his first news of the murders. He quickly went with his son, Justin Huntly, to the Westminster

Palace Hotel to meet Parnell, Davitt, Dillon, and Tim Healy (MP for Wexford). The sense of crisis was so great that Parnell and Healy both considered resigning from politics; and Justin Huntly McCarthy gave a revolver to Davitt, who feared a mob attack on the hotel. McCarthy later claimed that he was the first to oppose the resignation option and convince his colleagues to remain in parliament.

After the heightened tensions that followed the murders and the resultant Crime Act had abated, McCarthy found himself in the natural position of supporting a Liberal government. As strongly opposed to Conservative principles as he was committed to Liberal ideals, he nonetheless enjoyed the company of MPs on both sides of the House – including that of Tory maverick Lord Randolph Churchill.

After the 1880 general election, McCarthy and Churchill both sat on the Opposition benches, with McCarthy habitually sitting behind the unpredictable lord. They shared a love of literature and apparently a similar sense of humour. McCarthy thought Churchill displayed 'a curious combination of the school-boy and the statesman'[21] and, when the two men met one evening at a crowded reception in a London house, Churchill certainly gave rein to his prankish nature.

After they had exchanged pleasantries and were about to part, Churchill button-holed McCarthy and drew him into a corner. In hushed tones, he told McCarthy that a political gossip columnist was watching them, probably suspecting that they were 'concocting some tremendous political machination'.[22] Churchill suggested that they therefore continue to huddle in the corner, talking in undertones on any subject of McCarthy's choice. The latter saw the humour in the situation, and presumably did so again the next day, when some newspapers carried a report of the apparent political plotting taking place in public view. Although politics was for McCarthy an extremely serious business, it did also bring friendships and lighter moments and these, especially during the 1880s, certainly added to his enjoyment of Westminster.

In addition to his leading articles for the *Daily News*, and propaganda for the nationalist cause in journals such as the monthly *Nineteenth Century*,[23] McCarthy continued his literary output during the 1880s. After the success of *A History of Our Own Times* (which was translated into German in 1881 and French in 1885–7), there appeared in 1884 the substantial first volume of his *A History of the Four Georges*, covering the period 1714–33. He also collaborated on a number of novels with Australian-born author Rosa Praed, with whom he was to form one of the closest relationships of his life.

Rosa Caroline Murray-Prior was born in 1851, the daughter of a Queensland pastoralist and politician. In 1872 she married an Englishman, Arthur Campbell Buckley Praed, and four years later the couple moved to England. She later recalled her first meeting with McCarthy in the mid-1880s:

> There advanced, in a short-sighted manner, a slenderly built gentleman of modest mien, with a massive head and intellectual forehead, from which the reddish-grey hair rolled back in a sort of leonine wave . . . He wore a pince-nez: his manner was quiet and very courteous: he spoke in a soft voice with the slightest touch of brogue, and, during the talk at dinner, revealed himself in unobtrusive fashion as a highly polished, travelled and agreeable man of the world.[24]

McCarthy and Praed's literary collaboration included political novels such as *The Right Honourable* (1886) and *The Rebel Rose* (1888). Of greater long-term significance, however, were the regular – sometimes even daily – letters McCarthy wrote to Praed – 'my best friend'[25] – and the memoranda he dictated to her. Praed was, in certain regards, a substitute wife for McCarthy and, although it seems unlikely that their relationship ever became sexual, their emotional closeness makes these letters a valuable source for the biographer.

In June 1885 the Liberals were in disarray, and were defeated on a budget division in the Commons by the combined opposition of the Conservatives and the Irish Party. Developments that month marked 'the final emergence of Salisbury as uncontested leader of his party',[26] and he became Prime Minister as head of a minority Conservative government. In this unsettled situation, the Conservatives entered into negotiations with the Irish Party, the preliminary talks of which involved McCarthy and the new Irish viceroy, the Earl of Carnarvon.

McCarthy met Carnarvon in London in early July. In his *Reminiscences*, McCarthy recalled that at this meeting, 'Lord Carnarvon distinctly told me that for his own part he was prepared to go as far in the direction of Home Rule as either Parnell or I could desire.' Carnarvon made it clear that he spoke only for himself and not for his Cabinet colleagues. He did, however, hold out 'some hope of being able to bring over his colleagues to his own views on the subject'.[27] A subsequent meeting was arranged between Carnarvon and Parnell.

Although Parnell reported to McCarthy that the result of this second meeting had been 'only that each would do his best to bring about a satisfactory arrangement',[28] the Conservatives were to reap considerable short-term benefit from the Irish Party's decision to call on the Irish community in Britain to vote against the Liberals – and therefore effectively in favour of the Conservatives – at the general election in November 1885. This election was to prove significant for both the Irish Party and McCarthy personally.

Eighty-six pledge-bound Irish Party MPs, united behind one leader, were returned to parliament.[29] This result was a great victory for the Irish National League (the party's organisation), and for the policy of extracting a pledge from each candidate, before he received the League's nomination, that if elected he would 'sit, act and vote with the Irish parliamentary party'.[30] Another outcome of the election was the placing of Home Rule at the very centre of the Irish political stage, with the consequent polarisation of Irish politics along the lines of nationalist *versus* unionist. (The other Irish seats were won by 16 Conservatives and two independent Conservatives.)

The 1885 election was significant for McCarthy personally in that it was the first time he had fought an election contest. The 1884 Representation of the People Act (which trebled the Irish electorate) and the 1885 Redistribution of Seats Act meant that the expanded Ulster electorate now included a large number of labourers and Roman Catholics, and the Irish Party made a concerted effort to win seats in that province. Most of the party's candidates in Ulster were well-known figures, and McCarthy was chosen as its standard-bearer for Londonderry City.

His opponent was a Presbyterian, Charles Edward Lewis, who had been Conservative MP for the constituency since 1872. McCarthy seemed to enjoy the hustings, writing to Praed that, 'We hold rival meetings every night and my opponent and I abuse each other to our heart's content',[31] but he was constantly afraid of physical, as distinct from verbal, violence. In an earlier letter to Praed he had written that, 'So far, there has been perfect order, but I fear for the polling day if the rival crowds should meet.'[32] No violence erupted, however, and on 26 November Lewis won by 1,824 votes to McCarthy's 1,792.[33] After this narrow defeat, McCarthy travelled to North Longford, where the election took place on 2 December. In this safe seat he won a landslide victory, receiving 2,549 votes, compared to 163 votes for his Conservative opponent, James Mackay Wilson.[34] The general election proved a double victory for the McCarthy family, as McCarthy's son, Justin Huntly, was also elected – unopposed for Newry.

Together with the 86 Irish Party members, 334 Liberals and 250 Conservatives (who included the 18 Irish Conservatives mentioned earlier) were returned to the United Kingdom parliament and, although the Irish Party was strong enough to help keep the Liberals out of office, it was not sufficiently numerous to keep the Conservatives in power. In this fluid situation, the Irish Party continued to have talks with the Conservatives, who clung on to office.

McCarthy and Carnarvon met on 13 December and continued their private discussions. In an effort presumably to attract the Conservatives, McCarthy, according to Carnarvon, said that he distrusted Gladstone, who very likely 'wd. put them off, that disappointment wd. Ensue – & perhaps some wretched rising wd. take place'. Concerning the crucial question of a Home Rule legislature, Carnarvon noted that McCarthy 'accepted principle of a gradual development – of securities for religion and property – of a Colonial constitution – of Imperial Connection'. Regarding the type of legislature preferred, McCarthy 'said that a Parliament in name with comparatively few powers & many safeguards wd. be taken in lieu of something called a Board or Council with great powers & no restrictions on it'.[35]

How serious either side was in these discussions is open to conjecture. McCarthy later noted that during the course of the meeting Carnarvon 'took an opportunity of telling me that he had not been able to bring all his colleagues round to his way of thinking, and that, therefore, the negotiations, if I may call them so, had come to an end'.[36] Irrespective of whether or not discussions had finished at this point, the leaking on 17 December of what was alleged to be Gladstone's intentions for an Irish settlement, including the creation of an Irish parliament, finalised matters.

Later that month McCarthy met Churchill, now Secretary for India in Salisbury's government, who let McCarthy 'infer from what he said that his party thought they had no chance about Home Rule after Gladstone had taken it up and that they had therefore better drop it and take to the British Philistine view'.[37] The Irish Party could therefore no longer play the Conservatives against the Liberals. When parliament reassembled in late January 1886, the Irish Party combined with the latter, and on 1 February Gladstone began his third term as Prime Minister.

Between February and April 1886 McCarthy had a number of meetings with John Morley, the new Irish Chief Secretary, whom he had known since the 1860s. Morley had succeeded McCarthy as editor of the *Morning Star*, and had been the editor from 1867 to 1882 of the *Fortnightly Review*, organ of advanced liberalism, to which McCarthy had contributed.

Gladstone introduced his Government of Ireland Bill on 8 April 1886. It provided for an Irish parliament, with an Irish executive, responsible to the legislative body. The multitudinous limitations specified in the bill made explicit the areas, such as the crown, war, and customs and excise, over which the Irish parliament would have no authority. Despite all these restrictions, the Irish Party was still prepared to support the measure. McCarthy, speaking on 21 May during the second reading, while referring to the need for modifications to the bill, stated that he and his colleagues accepted it in principle

> because it is a measure for the self-government of Ireland – because for the first time since the Union, a great Minister and a great Party have raised the national flag of Irish self-government. In that spirit, and with that in view, we cordially accept the Bill which proposes to give us a Parliament on College Green.

During this speech McCarthy showed his debating skills to good advantage. Addressing himself to the contentious question of whether Irish MPs should continue to sit in the Commons after an Irish parliament had been established (a number of English members threatened to oppose the bill if some Irish MPs did not continue to sit at Westminster), he impishly said that

> It is surely most delightful and flattering to us to be told that we are the keystone of the Imperial arch. Yes; it now appears that once we are withdrawn this splendid structure falls to pieces. Our opinion of ourselves grows every day. We never knew we were such nice people before. We never knew in what tender affection we were held. We never knew what pleasant company we are, and what tears would be shed at our departure.[38]

No tears had to be shed. Although the party, with the sole exception of O'Shea, voted for the second reading on 7 June, the measure was still defeated – by 341 votes to 311, with 93 Liberals voting against.

McCarthy was not unduly disappointed by the defeat. He wrote that night to Praed, 'We are defeated, my colleague . . . Never mind! . . . we'll soon win. Gladstone's speech splendid. Great scene at Division.'[39] Having been defeated on such a central issue, Gladstone called a general election.

On 5 July 1886 McCarthy contested his second Londonderry City election, where he once again faced Lewis, now running as a Unionist. McCarthy presumably received the support of all of the Roman Catholic voters, and about 30 Presbyterian Liberals. (It was claimed that Gladstone had written personal letters to some 20 Londonderry Liberals asking them to vote for McCarthy.) The result of the election was 1,781 votes for Lewis, and 1,778 for McCarthy.[40] Writing to Praed he said, 'I am well content . . . We have reduced the Orange majority to three; and I am assured that on petition we shall win the seat.'[41] (This close result led to the temporary nickname, 'Justout' McCarthy.) Although he also stood for North Longford, where he was returned unopposed on 8 July,[42] McCarthy later petitioned against alleged Unionist illegality in the Londonderry election.

The July 1886 election, fought on the single issue of Home Rule for Ireland, was a disaster for the Prime Minister. While the Irish Party remained practically unchanged with 85 seats, the Liberals were reduced from 334 to 191. Salisbury now formed another government and remained in office for six years. The loss of power was not, however, the only significant result for the Liberals; another 'was a great purge of the party and a drastic simplification of Liberal politics'. Henceforth 'the "true Liberal" was now to be defined and identified on the basis of support for Gladstone's Home Rule policy'.[43]

In September 1886 McCarthy began a lecture tour of the United States and Canada. As the 'accredited envoy of the Irish Parliamentary party',[44] his arrival in America received significant press coverage. Over the next six months he delivered some one hundred lectures (not including banquet speeches and replies to addresses), speaking chiefly on 'The Cause of Ireland'. He also met old friends and made new acquaintances, including Edward Blake (the leader of the opposition in the Canadian parliament), and visited the White House, where he met President Grover Cleveland.

Despite the new and renewed friendships, McCarthy did not enjoy the tour. As this was an 'official' visit, he was constantly in demand, and from early on he was 'sick of playing the part of great public man'.[45] There was, furthermore, the tedium of the endless winter travel. He wrote to Praed that, 'The long monotonous daily journeys through a country made uniform with the snow ... [are] wearying to a degree which you would hardly understand.'[46] He did derive some personal satisfaction from the trip, however, as he considered he had brought the 'cause . . . to the understanding of Americans whom other Irishmen perhaps could not reach so well'.[47]

Before going to America McCarthy had, on legal advice, declined to take his seat for North Longford, pending an appeal regarding the Londonderry contest. On petition, Lewis was unseated owing to electoral irregularities, and McCarthy, back in England in March 1887, took his seat as member for Londonderry City. Later that month the newly appointed Irish Chief Secretary, Arthur Balfour (Salisbury's nephew), introduced his Criminal Law Amendment Bill into the Commons – and Irish Party MPs soon discovered that Balfour's 'languid manner disguised a fitfully firm resolve'.[48] With his appointment, 'the whole tenor of Government policy in Ireland changed, and for the first time the Parnellites faced an adversary willing to fight fire with fire'.[49] Balfour's crimes bill was the government's response to both the unofficial Plan of Campaign (to force down rents paid to landlords) and spontaneous agrarian disturbances, as falling prices meant that tenants could not pay their rents, and consequently evictions and disturbances increased. Despite strenuous opposition from the Irish Party and the Liberals, the bill became law in mid-July 1887.

As well as this political setback, McCarthy was facing personal problems, and by the summer of 1887 he was considering retiring from politics on medical grounds. Now 56, the combined strain of his political and literary careers had begun to tell, and in July he offered Parnell his resignation. Parnell, however, persuaded him to postpone his decision. From March to June 1887, *The Times* had been running a series of articles under the general heading of 'Parnellism and Crime'. In this heated atmosphere, Parnell insisted that McCarthy's proposed departure from politics would be seen as 'not resignation, but repudiation . . . for reasons which

[McCarthy] would not publicly state'. Parnell also warned of the effect of a resignation at that time on the English people in general and on Gladstone in particular, and of the likely replacement of McCarthy as vice-chairman by 'some extreme man'.[50]

Accepting the validity of Parnell's arguments, McCarthy agreed to remain as vice-chairman, and continued to be busy both inside and outside of parliament. While colleagues such as William O'Brien and John Dillon led the Plan of Campaign in Ireland, McCarthy's activities included involvement in Liberal by-election campaigns in England. Thus, while some party colleagues were further developing their popular reputations in Ireland, McCarthy was seen as the acceptable face of Irish Nationalism in England.[51]

Political contact with the Liberals – the 'union of hearts' – went hand-in-hand with social events, such as an invitation to dine with Gladstone, which McCarthy considered 'a curious illustration of the change in the times'.[52] Not all invitations were accepted. A request to join the House of Commons 1887 Jubilee Committee, to celebrate the golden jubilee of Queen Victoria's accession to the throne, was declined. While not intending any disrespect to the sovereign, McCarthy considered that 'when Ireland's share in the Jubilee is a coercion bill, a prominent Irish member holding a sort of official position in the Irish Party, would seem hardly in his right place on a Jubilee committee'.[53]

A year after Balfour's Criminal Law & Procedure (Ireland) Act was passed, Salisbury's government established a Special Commission in mid-1888 to examine the charges levelled against Parnell and his colleagues by *The Times*, in its 1887 articles on 'Parnellism and Crime'. When in February 1889 Richard Pigott, a journalist, blackmailer, and dealer in pornography, confessed to having forged the letters upon which *The Times* had based its case, Parnell and his colleagues were vindicated in the popular mind. By coincidence, McCarthy was at this time facing legal difficulties of his own.

On Christmas Day 1888, while on holiday in Algiers, McCarthy wrote to Praed that he had been served with a writ for debts arising from an Irish Exhibition. This Exhibition had opened in London in June 1888 and McCarthy, along with others, had joined the executive council of the Exhibition, 'on the assurance that we were incurring no pecuniary liability whatever',[54] in order to assist the enterprise. By November 1888 when it closed, the Exhibition had incurred a substantial debt, for which the members of the executive council were, to McCarthy's surprise, later held personally liable. The cases dragged on, with McCarthy hoping that the Exhibition's creditors would make a significant reduction in their bill, in order to arrange a speedy payment, and that he would 'be able to meet this Exhibition trouble myself, without the help of the Irish Party or anyone'.[55]

Throughout the Special Commission and the Irish Exhibition cases, McCarthy continued to campaign for Liberal candidates at by-elections, and he maintained a regular attendance at parliament. He also made himself available to speak for causes he believed to be deserving of support, including the suffering of women workers in the East End of London, and the grievances of Indian civil servants. In addition, he was prepared to write articles for a nominal fee if he felt a journal and its readers deserved support, and Irish Party affairs continued to demand his attention outside of the Commons.

During this period, McCarthy had two opportunities that could significantly have altered the direction of his political life. He declined both. In February 1888 he was invited by the Speaker to become one of five men who, under new rules, would preside as Deputy Chairmen in the House, in the absence of the Speaker or the paid Chairman of Committees. His colleagues were divided on whether or not he should accept a Deputy Chairmanship. T. P. O'Connor felt he should, as to do so 'would have been a complete vindication of our party'. William O'Brien, on the other hand, counselled against acceptance. McCarthy declined the offer, writing to Praed that he 'couldn't allow [himself] to be brought within reasonable distance of paid office in political times like these'. There was perhaps some regret, not necessarily personal, when he told her that five men had been appointed – with 'no Irishman among them'.[56]

McCarthy also declined Parnell's offer, made in April 1888, to become the managing director of the *Freeman's Journal*. McCarthy considered it 'the best unofficial position a man could have in Ireland', and that 'in the worldly and practical sense there is much to be said for it'. He had, however, no intention of accepting, as 'it would mean living in Ireland all the recess and going there very often during the session'.[57] Prepared to devote his life to helping Ireland, he was not prepared to live there.

McCarthy therefore continued as a journalist and author in London. He wrote obituary and regular leader articles for the *Daily News*, and completed the second volume of his *A History of the Four Georges* in October 1889. His writings were not, however, generating sufficient income. In early 1890 he was 'living from hand to mouth' and was compelled to accept invitations to write 'pot-boilers'. The need for instant income meant that he had to 'turn day after day, and week after week from the work which would perhaps be really profitable in the future to the work which pays something or anything in the present'.[58]

Financial worries notwithstanding, in August 1890 McCarthy was also contemplating life after Home Rule had been achieved. 'When we have a Liberal Ministry and a Home Rule Parliament in Ireland,' he wrote, 'I might be offered office here or there . . . Or I might be offered some foreign or colonial appointment from a

Liberal Government.' He had, however, two reservations about such schemes. The first was whether it would suit him to lose his independence; the second, whether these offers would ever come to fruition – 'schemes which any accident, any breath may lay in the dust and reduce to nothing'.[59] Four months later this was precisely what happened.

McCarthy spent the 1889 Christmas holiday in Cannes, and there heard the news that William O'Shea was suing his wife for divorce, naming Parnell as co-respondent. Eleven months later, in November 1890, the case came to court. The events of the period 17 November to 6 December 1890 – from the divorce court decision against Katharine O'Shea and Parnell, to the split of the party and McCarthy's election to its chairmanship – are well known and are discussed in detail in other studies.[60] In view of their consequences for McCarthy, and the widespread but erroneous belief that he had been aware – but had failed to inform Parnell and the Irish Party – of Gladstone's threat to resign if Parnell did not do so, it is necessary to outline McCarthy's role over these twenty days.

On 17 November 1890, after two days of uncontested hearings, O'Shea obtained a decree *nisi* of divorce. Even before the announcement, McCarthy had been devising a political strategy for the new situation. Concerned about the possible effects of the case on both the party and its leadership, he had decided that the best policy would be to ignore the court's verdict. 'We ought', he wrote on 16 November, 'to do nothing and take no notice – simply go on as we are constantly doing in Parnell's absence – not make any even temporary change in the leadership – not take the public into our confidence at all – go on and say nothing as a party about the whole matter. It will all soon blow over.'[61]

There may have been some wishful thinking in this prediction. The previous January, while coming to terms with the news that Parnell had been cited in the divorce case, he had admitted to

Praed that he 'was struck with positive consternation'. This was partially because, if Parnell were to retire from public life, McCarthy (as vice-chairman) reluctantly considered himself to be the likely replacement.

> I am not equal to the leadership in health or means or leisure or spirits and yet, if I refuse, the papers all will say that I was getting sick of the whole thing. I feel frightfully upset by the affair.[62]

On 16 November McCarthy had good reason to believe that his policy of ignoring the court's verdict might work. Parnell was above all a survivor. In the 1870s as a newly elected MP, he had survived attacks by Butt; and in the 1880s he had survived the fallout from the Phoenix Park murders, and the subsequent allegations in *The Times*. McCarthy presumably felt that, if the party presented a united front behind the leader, it could and would overcome any opposition. This view that Parnell could remain as leader was shared by John Morley. In a letter to Sir William Harcourt, a senior Liberal Party colleague, Morley wrote, 'I regard it as certain that the Irish will not throw him [Parnell] over in any case, and if they don't, nobody else can.'[63]

In Dublin on 20 November for a previously scheduled public meeting, 24 members of the Irish Party were present when McCarthy, in the chair, proposed the successful motion:

> That this meeting, interpreting the sentiment of the Irish people that no side issue shall be permitted to obstruct the progress of the great cause of home rule for Ireland, declares that in all political matters Mr Parnell possesses the confidence of the Irish nation, and rejoices at the determination of the Irish parliamentary party to stand by their leader.[64]

This motion clearly distinguished between the private matter of the divorce and the public issue of Home Rule. Unfortunately for

McCarthy, the English Nonconformists drew no such distinction, and made their views abundantly clear at the National Liberal Federation's annual meeting on 20 and 21 November. The Nonconformists had been solidly behind Gladstone since the 1860s, and their support was considered vital. Their decision, that the Liberals must cease co-operation with the Irish Party if Parnell remained as leader, was conveyed to Gladstone by Harcourt, who stressed that the future of the Liberal Party was at stake. What the Nonconformists did not know was that Gladstone had been aware, since May 1882, of Parnell's relationship with Katharine O'Shea. Nor did they know that Gladstone had met Mrs O'Shea privately in a London hotel on more than one occasion, shortly after he was informed of the affair.[65]

After the views of the Nonconformists became known, there followed an exchange of letters and a series of meetings among senior Liberal figures. Gladstone now decided that two means of communication should be used to convey the Liberals' position to Parnell, who had been out of reach since the divorce court's decision. The first involved a meeting between Gladstone and McCarthy on 24 November – the eve of both the opening of parliament, and the annual selection of the sessional chairman of the Irish Party. The second means was a letter from Gladstone addressed to Morley, which recorded Gladstone's views and was intended to be shown to Parnell before the latter met his parliamentary colleagues on 25 November.

Morley, in his influential 1903 authorised biography of Gladstone, makes only a passing reference to the Gladstone–McCarthy meeting. His single-sentence comment states that, 'The same evening Mr McCarthy was placed in possession of Mr Gladstone's views, to be laid before Mr Parnell at the earliest moment.'[66] What precisely those views were, Morley left unstated. McCarthy, however, did not. That evening he wrote to Praed, telling her that

Gladstone had informed him 'very sadly that [Parnell] remaining in the leadership now means the loss of the next elections and the putting off of Home Rule until a time when he (Gladstone) will no longer be able to bear a hand in the great struggle to which he has devoted the last years of his life'. McCarthy told Praed that Gladstone had authorised him to convey his (Gladstone's) views to Parnell.[67] McCarthy had left the meeting, he later told Praed, 'under the impression . . . that, though he [Gladstone] disapproved of Parnell, he would still fight for our cause'.[68] The possibility of Gladstone resigning was never mentioned.

Gladstone's second means of communication was his letter to Morley. This was written after his meeting with McCarthy, and Gladstone agreed to include a reference to his own possible resignation (if Parnell refused to resign) only at Morley's insistence.[69] As Gladstone had failed to inform McCarthy of his own threatened resignation, just as he had omitted the threat from his draft letter, it is clear that it was Gladstone himself, and not McCarthy, who was responsible for the confusion over Gladstone's intended action. The much-repeated charge that McCarthy failed to convey the resignation message to Parnell cannot stand. He did not relay Gladstone's resignation threat, for the very simple reason that Gladstone had never mentioned it. McCarthy's version of events has since been accepted as likely, with the editor of Gladstone's diaries writing, 'McCarthy probably did not know of a further point, added to the letter at John Morley's prompting', i.e. Gladstone's threatened resignation.[70]

In a life as long and as public as Gladstone's, it is not surprising that incidents of confusion can be cited. What is surprising is that in great set-pieces, pre-planned as they were, confusion should ensue. Gladstone had invited McCarthy to their meeting on 24 November, and had had time to plan in advance exactly what he wanted to say, and what message he wanted to convey. It appears that, without Morley's assistance, i.e. in re-drafting the letter, he was unable to do so.

This was not the first occasion on which clarity of expression failed Gladstone at an important juncture, and it cannot be explained away by reference to his considerable age (he would be 81 the following month). A much earlier example of his failure to explain his ideas clearly had occurred in 1845, when he was resigning from Sir Robert Peel's Conservative administration over the Maynooth question.

The details of that question need not concern us. What is important, however, is the confusion that surrounded Gladstone's decision to resign. What a modern historian has called Gladstone's 'convoluted explanation' of his thinking confused, rather than enlightened, at least some of those with whom he shared his views.[71] In January 1845 Peel, referring to a letter he had received from Gladstone, wrote to a colleague, 'I take it for granted . . . that the letter means to announce his continued intention to retire.' Peel was forced to admit that 'I really have great difficulty sometimes in exactly comprehending what Gladstone means.'[72] The following month, after Gladstone had announced his resignation in the House of Commons, John Cam Hobhouse, the future Lord Broughton, having listened to Gladstone's statement, wrote, 'although it was not quite . . . unintelligible, . . . Why the deuce did he quit the Cabinet? Everyone asks this.'[73]

Gladstone's meeting with McCarthy in November 1890, like his resignation from Peel's government 45 years earlier, was a planned event – not a spur of the moment decision – and yet on each occasion confusion abounded. It is little wonder, therefore, that McCarthy left Gladstone's residence in Carlton Gardens with one interpretation of events, while Gladstone, later that evening – with Morley's subsequent assistance – claimed another. It seems reasonable to assume that 'a mixture of Gladstone's changing mood and his irredeemable opaqueness may have disrupted communications in these crucial hours and days'.[74]

The rest is well known. McCarthy met Parnell shortly before the planned party meeting, relayed to him his (McCarthy's) understanding of Gladstone's views,[75] and Parnell was subsequently re-elected chairman for the forthcoming session. In view of the threatened revolt by the Nonconformists, Gladstone, a consummate politician, as soon as he heard of Parnell's re-election, protected his electoral base and insisted upon immediate publication of his ostensibly private letter to Morley.

The publication of this letter brought the Irish Party into a state of crisis. McCarthy was as surprised as his colleagues to learn of Gladstone's intentions. 'We have new complications', McCarthy wrote that evening to Praed, 'Gladstone threatens to resign if Parnell will not – this came out to-night.'[76] McCarthy now told his Irish Party colleagues of Gladstone's communication to him which, he reported, he had previously relayed to Parnell. When Parnell refused to summon a new meeting of the party, 31 members, including McCarthy, convened one by requisition. McCarthy was now in no doubt that Parnell would have to go. The next day he sent a telegram to Praed: 'Am going thoroughly with Gladstone.'[77]

McCarthy's preferred solution was for Parnell to accept voluntary retirement, at least for a temporary period, as a forced retirement would probably split the party and endanger the Liberal alliance. McCarthy was also motivated by private concerns: he and Parnell had been friends since the 1870s, and he had no wish 'to vote for the dethroning of Parnell, for whom [he] had so much public devotion and private friendship!'[78] Despite these personal reservations, he began preparing for Parnell's forced removal as chairman.

On 27 November McCarthy persuaded Parnell to delay the issuing of his proposed manifesto to the Irish people, and used this period to have two meetings with Gladstone. On 29 November the manifesto was published. Besides questioning 'the integrity and independence' of some of Parnell's party colleagues, it also contained an account of a confidential discussion between Parnell and Gladstone, which had taken place the previous December at the latter's home at Hawarden. The message of this selective and misleading manifesto was that Gladstone and the Liberals were not to be trusted on the issue of Home Rule.[79] McCarthy, through his meetings with Gladstone before the publication of the manifesto, managed to limit its impact on the Liberals, and in return received assurances of Gladstone's continued support.

Seventy-three party members were present at the reconvened Irish Party meeting in Committee Room 15, on Monday 1 December. In the face of mounting opposition, Parnell was bound to be deposed by a vote of the majority of the party. From America, William O'Brien and John Dillon wired to McCarthy that 'Mr Parnell's continued leadership is impossible.'[80] From Ireland, having remained unusually quiet on the divorce issue, Thomas William Croke, Roman Catholic archbishop of Cashel, telegraphed McCarthy, 'All sorry for Parnell but still in God's name let him retire quietly.'[81] Faced with the prospect of certain removal, Parnell abused his position as chairman and for six days refused to allow a vote on a motion proposing the ending of his chairmanship.

At the 1 December meeting, the leading party figures present made their main contributions to the debate. McCarthy attacked Parnell for the manner in which he had handled the Hawarden discussions. Purporting to accept at face value Parnell's version of events, McCarthy said that Parnell had made too little of his error of keeping private until then that conversation with Gladstone. Parnell had, McCarthy said, 'possessed a secret vital to the cause' of Ireland, and yet he had refused to reveal it because of a pledge. No such pledge should have been given, McCarthy argued, but, if it had been given and if Parnell had consequently been bound to silence, then he was not bound publicly to commend Gladstone, knowing 'that Mr Gladstone's purpose was, if he could, to betray the Irish cause and Irish people'.

Furthermore, McCarthy continued, if this bond of silence ('that seal as rigid as the seal of the confessional itself') were to be broken, it should have been revealed at an earlier time, 'when it might have been of great service by warning Irishmen against false friends', rather than being sprung upon the party and country in a manifesto. The whole transaction 'betrayed from the beginning a vital error of judgment'. Determined to have Parnell deposed, McCarthy told him that this error 'imperilled and must always imperil, your leadership and work', and that he (McCarthy) could not see 'any hope, if the present arrangement of the party should last, that the cause of the country is to be served and saved'.[82] McCarthy considered it to be a simple choice between Parnell and the Home Rule cause – and he could no longer support Parnell.

'Few more arrogant demands have ever been presented to a people', writes Joseph Lee, 'than Parnell's insistence that Ireland abandon all chance of apparently imminent home rule simply to maintain his leadership.'[83] For a further four days Parnell avoided the motion on the chairmanship, as he and his supporters strove for tactical advantage in the face of strengthening opposition. After a meeting of the Roman Catholic hierarchy's standing committee on 3 December, this opposition included the Roman Catholic bishops of Ireland.

From Wednesday 3 December, much of the debate inside Committee Room 15 revolved around the attempts by Parnell to gain assurances from Gladstone and his party colleagues about the provisions of a future Home Rule Bill, regarding control of the constabulary and the settlement of the land question. On 5 December, when Gladstone refused to deal further with the Irish

Party until it resolved the leadership question 'in such a manner as will enable me to renew former relations',[84] the party was forced to choose between, on the one hand, Gladstone and probable Home Rule; and, on the other, Parnell and the end of the vital Liberal alliance.

On Saturday 6 December, after further procedural disputes, Parnell at last allowed the motion proposing his removal as chairman to be put to the meeting. Once put, however, he declared it out of order, and a heated argument ensued. McCarthy now rose and, as predetermined, protested at Parnell's conduct and called on his colleagues to withdraw *en masse* from the meeting. Having regretted that Parnell had lent little assistance to resolving 'this national crisis', McCarthy said that there was

> no further use carrying on a discussion which must be barren of all but reproach, ill-temper, controversy, and indignity, and I will therefore suggest that all who think with me at this grave crisis should withdraw with me from this room.[85]

McCarthy and 44 colleagues then walked out of the Committee Room, leaving Parnell behind with 27 supporters.

McCarthy and his colleagues immediately proceeded to business. Reassembling in a conference room nearby, within fifteen minutes they had declared Parnell's chairmanship to be terminated; had elected McCarthy as sessional chairman; had resolved shortly to elect a committee of eight members to rule the party in conjunction with the chairman; and, having reaffirmed the principle that the Irish Party must remain independent of all other parties, declared that they would accept only a Home Rule proposal that satisfied the aspirations of the Irish people.

A period of political civil war was about to break out in Ireland.

CHAPTER 4

Reluctant Chairman, 1890–6

McCarthy was a reluctant chairman. He reluctantly led the majority of his colleagues out of Committee Room 15, and he reluctantly accepted and retained the position of sessional chairman of the Irish Party. Despite poor health and major personal financial hardship, he held that position from December 1890 to February 1896.

It was important for the future of constitutional politics in Ireland that he do so. The once monolithic Irish Party had split in two, and the McCarthy-led Irish Party had an uncomfortably small majority over its former colleagues, now rivals – the Parnellites. The party was consequently politically weak; it lacked an organisation and a daily newspaper (the Parnellites had 'captured' the Irish National League and the *Freeman's Journal*); and it was short of money. Apart from the financial issue, the others were short-term problems.

A more long-term problem was that of internal rivalries, which once more threatened to split the party. Through his conciliatory approach, and as the one leader under whom the rival factions could agree to serve, McCarthy ensured that there was no such split; the alliance with the Liberals continued; Gladstone's second Home Rule Bill was passed by the Commons; and constitutional politics retained majority support in Ireland.

In the short term there was open political conflict in Ireland. On 8 December 1890 the writ for the North Kilkenny by-election was moved, and the battle transferred from Committee Room 15 to Ireland. McCarthy played little direct part in this progressively bitter campaign – which was directed on the Irish Party side by Healy and Davitt – and instead concentrated on national issues. On 11 December the newspapers carried his strongly worded manifesto to the Irish people. In this, he clearly stated that the party was committed to the cause of Ireland, rather than to one man, Parnell.[1]

McCarthy did not, however, remain completely aloof from electioneering, and he did pay a brief visit to Ireland at this time. In Cork, he and his colleagues were 'howled at as enemies where we used to be blessed as friends', but he rejoiced that 'the whole intelligence of the people is with us and we have done wonderfully well'.[2] Verbal abuse continued when he went to North Kilkenny for the by-election. One of Parnell's less-extreme comments during that election campaign was his much-quoted description of McCarthy as 'a nice old gent for a tea party'.[3] Verbal insult was soon followed by physical violence, and both Davitt and Parnell were assaulted before the campaign ended on 22 December. The result was a win for the Irish Party over the Parnellites, by 2,527 votes to 1,362.

This was a crucial victory for the Irish Party, and the margin was a source of comfort to McCarthy who wrote that, 'It may scatter the Parnellite hopes and . . . stop this odious civil war.'[4] Despite the result, and subsequent wins by the party at by-elections in North Sligo in April and Carlow in June 1891 (the latter by a margin of over 2,200 votes), the Parnellites were not scattered and the conflict continued in Ireland. It was therefore necessary for the party to establish a new newspaper and party machine.

On 7 March 1891 the first edition of the party's new daily newspaper, the *National Press*, was published. It was considered vital that it be quickly produced, as a counterbalance to the

Parnellite *Freeman's Journal*. In February McCarthy had written
that 'we fight at a great disadvantage with no paper to give our
views and back us up'.[5] No time was wasted once the *National Press*
was launched, and on 10 March McCarthy addressed an audience
of 1,500 at the inaugural meeting of the Irish National Federation
in Dublin. The Federation was the Irish Party's answer to the
Parnellite-controlled Irish National League. McCarthy, as sessional chairman of the Irish Party, became *ex-officio* president of
the council of the new Federation.

As well as establishing a new newspaper and a new organisation,
McCarthy had to ensure the continued unity of the party. To do so,
it was important to secure the support of William O'Brien and
John Dillon, both of whom returned from America and entered
into separate negotiations, conducted in France, with McCarthy
and with Parnell. In mid-January 1891, to McCarthy's distress,
O'Brien was 'unconsciously and in honest good faith helping to
play the game of "Committee Room 15" all over again'.[6]

During these talks, held in Boulogne, McCarthy's approach
was firm but non-committal. As he wrote to Healy, 'We simply say
that we can do nothing without the knowledge and consent of the
Party – which we maintain to be *the* Party'. Referring to Parnell's
stipulation that his (Parnell's) deposition should be regarded as
invalid, McCarthy wrote that any discussion of the validity of the
proceeding was 'inadmissible', and that he considered the proposal
that he resign his own position, in order to placate Parnell, to be a
matter for his 55 MP colleagues to decide.[7]

When the Boulogne negotiations ended in failure on 11
February 1891, O'Brien and Dillon, who had evaded their police
shadows and fled the United Kingdom in early October 1890 (in
order to avoid a prison sentence under Balfour's coercion act),
crossed to England. There, they were promptly arrested and sent
to Galway jail, where they were incarcerated until the end of July

1891. On their release they travelled to London, where they met McCarthy on 4 August. Five days later, their public siding with the Irish Party against the Parnellites meant that the party was strengthened and its unity maintained.

The maintenance of the Liberal alliance was of almost equal importance to McCarthy. The Irish Party had split over this issue in December 1890 and, from that time on, he was in regular communication with Gladstone, and even more so with Morley. This close cooperation brought undoubted political benefits to McCarthy and the Irish Party, and in late January 1891 the Liberal leaders gave McCarthy assurances regarding land and the constabulary, and the inclusion of these issues in any forthcoming Home Rule legislation.

This was the Liberal alliance in action. During the Committee Room 15 meetings, Parnell had repeatedly told his colleagues that they should not remove him unless the Liberals were to give assurances on future Home Rule provisions concerning these matters. The January 1891 assurances, which McCarthy was permitted to make public after the Boulogne negotiations had broken down, showed, he told Praed, 'that we could have got and will get all from the Liberals that we asked them to give us'.[8]

In 1891, while political matters were progressing reasonably satisfactorily, McCarthy's personal financial affairs were in disarray. During January he appeared in court regarding the Irish Exhibition cases, which he lost. On 13 February he wrote to Praed that, 'I paid away all the money I had, to meet the costs of the Irish Exhibition so far.'[9] During the summer, further cases were decided against McCarthy and his Irish Exhibition associates, which resulted in his incurring a debt of £2,000 (equivalent to over £207,000 in current value).[10] Although personally unable to produce this sum, McCarthy was not prepared to appeal for financial assistance. (In 1883 a financially embarrassed Parnell had accepted a national testimonial of £37,000 – almost £3.67 million in current value.[11]) McCarthy was therefore forced to avail of an offer made by his publisher, Chatto, to finance the debt, in return for his sacrificing the copyright of his *A History of Our Own Times*, and undertaking to write a novel without payment. In addition to the monetary setback – from which he never recovered – there was a concomitant detrimental effect on his health. This was a result of the long hours he was forced to work, in an effort to gain back some of the income he had lost in his well-meaning but naïve attempt to help Irish industry.

Throughout this time McCarthy had to make a living as a journalist and author, writing for the *Daily News* or producing 'pot-boilers'. The latter he found distasteful, 'Good Heavens!' he exclaimed to Praed, 'if I were a man of *any* means I would not write one single line that had not the inspiration of my own feeling and the approval of my own judgement.'[12] The Irish Exhibition debt meant, however, that he had no choice but to accept this unsatisfactory means of making a living.

The autumn of 1891 brought personal sadness, and a new political situation, with the unexpected death of Parnell on 6 October. Since the split the previous year, McCarthy and Parnell had remained on relatively good personal terms. Parnell had even composed his November 1890 manifesto 'To the people of Ireland' at a side table in McCarthy's presence, after they had dined together at the house of J. G. Fitzgerald, MP for South Longford.[13]

O'Brien recalled meeting McCarthy and Parnell together in mid-1891, in the Lobby of the House of Commons, after O'Brien's release from Galway jail. When O'Brien said that they were an unlikely trio to meet, Parnell said, 'with one of his softest smiles, "Justin and I have been over to the City together . . . to the admiration of all beholders."'[14] McCarthy and Parnell last met when the latter visited McCarthy at his 'house in London only three weeks before his [Parnell's] death'.[15]

The sudden death of his friend and former leader 'over-whelmed' McCarthy. On hearing of Parnell's death, McCarthy wrote to Praed, 'what friendship I had for him – how loyal I was to him, while loyalty was possible'. He then added 'what a shock it was for me when loyalty was no longer possible, and I had to face the hard facts and turn resolutely away from him'. McCarthy had to make himself available, the day the news of Parnell's death broke, to meet scores of 'interviewers from English and American newspapers . . . and [say] the same formal platitudes to each'. It was, he said, a 'tragic business.'[16]

Increasing demands on his time in early 1892 meant that even pot-boilers (a limited but crucial source of income) had to be set aside, as McCarthy devoted himself on an almost full-time basis to political affairs. A general election could not be long postponed, and he was therefore involved in regular attendance at the House. In March 1892 he wrote to Praed, 'I live in the House – if that can be called living.'[17] The expected dissolution of parliament took place at the end of June that year, and a general election followed in July.

In terms of seats won, the 1892 general election was a compre-hensive victory for the Irish Party, who won 71 out of the 103 Irish seats.[18] The Irish Unionist Parliamentary Party won 19 seats; the Parnellites, nine; and the Liberal Unionists, four. The 71 to nine victory for the Irish Party was somewhat flattering, as their Parnellite opponents secured around one-third of the nationalist vote. The first-past-the-post electoral system, however, resulted in an over-whelming victory for the Irish Party, in terms of seats won. Allowing for the inequality of the electoral system used – where votes received nationally did not equate to seats won – gaining the backing of two-thirds of the nationalist electorate was still a clear result. It showed that an indisputable majority of the Irish people continued to support McCarthy's Irish Party policy of an indepen-dent party, in close alliance with Gladstone's Liberal Party, dedicated to the achievement of Home Rule for Ireland.

McCarthy stood for re-election for Londonderry City, where his Irish Unionist Parliamentary Party opponent was John Ross. The latter was a local-born son of a Presbyterian minister, a graduate of Trinity College Dublin, and a Queen's Counsel. Ross recalled that he had 'received an urgent message . . . requesting [him] to come and see [Arthur Balfour] in . . . [Dublin] Castle'. The Chief Secretary there informed the Queen's Counsel that 'the Unionists of the city of Londonderry had demanded that [he] should be sent to eject Mr Justin McCarthy, if possible.' Ross later wrote that, 'Derry is about the hardest-fought seat in the Kingdom; it is where the two great tides meet, the old Anglo-Scottish colony on the one hand, and the great Celtic county of Donegal on the other.' In these tense conditions he 'arranged with the enemy, who were very friendly and most courteous, never to have our meetings on the same night, as if the excited crowds had come into collision, there would have been a desperate riot'.[19]

For health reasons, McCarthy was unable to campaign in person and lost the election on 7 July, with Ross polling 1,986 votes to McCarthy's 1,960.[20] This was a creditable performance, in the face of a strong local candidate and a presumed reluctance among liberal Protestants (who had been so important to McCarthy's election in 1886) to support a candidate from a party that, since Parnell's deposition, was seen to be coming increasingly under the influence of the Roman Catholic hierarchy. Following his narrow defeat in Londonderry, McCarthy won a landslide victory in North Longford on 15 July. Here he again faced his Conservative Party opponent from 1885, James Mackay Wilson, now representing the Unionist Party. This time, McCarthy won by 2,741 votes to 203.[21]

The future of Home Rule for Ireland depended as much on the result of the elections in Great Britain as those in Ireland. In the new House of Commons, 274 British Liberals and 81 Irish Nationalists (including the nine Parnellites) faced 268 Conservatives (including

19 Irish Unionists) and 47 Liberal Unionists (including four from Ireland). The result gave Gladstone at best a majority of only 40 in a House of 670 members.[22]

Gladstone – now leading his fourth and final administration – had sought a clear mandate for his programme, which prioritised Home Rule, and he was shocked by the Liberals' failure to win an overall majority. Initially, he thought of simply seeking to secure the assent of the House of Commons to the principle of Home Rule, as such a slim Commons majority meant that he was in a weak position to force through major constitutional change, especially in the face of certain rebuttal by the House of Lords. His senior colleagues, Harcourt (Chancellor of the Exchequer) and Lord Rosebery (Foreign Secretary), favoured such an approach. Morley (Chief Secretary for Ireland), however, was of the view that, 'The Irish are our masters and we had better realise it'.[23] Morley was backed by Earl Spencer (First Lord of the Admiralty), and Gladstone eventually committed himself to a second Home Rule Bill.

In late November 1892 Gladstone agreed to form an Irish Committee within the cabinet but, as in 1886, he kept his colleagues largely unaware of his detailed thinking regarding his proposed Home Rule legislation. Key figures such as Harcourt were excluded from the committee. In February 1893 two future Liberal prime ministers, Rosebery and H. H. Asquith, were in communication with one another on the subject of Home Rule. Asquith (now Home Secretary) informed Rosebery that a bill to amend the provisions for the Government of Ireland, which neither of them had seen, was about to be introduced into the Commons. Asquith ironically suggested that Rosebery 'may possibly like to be present, and hear what Her Majesty's Government have to propose'.[24]

In 1892 and 1893 the Irish Party, on the other hand, was in negotiations with John Morley (once more in Dublin Castle), over the contents of the proposed bill. McCarthy was in Dublin in early

November 1892 for marathon committee meetings, interrupted by daily exchanges of views with Morley. Negotiations continued in early 1893 in London, with Morley speaking for Gladstone, and McCarthy – accompanied by two of John Dillon, Thomas Sexton, and Edward Blake – negotiating for the Irish Party. (Blake had left Canada in 1892 and had been elected MP for South Longford at the general election that year.) In February 1893 McCarthy wrote to Praed that he was 'at present frozen into a mere politician. I am swallowed up in politics'.[25]

Outstanding difficulties remained when Gladstone introduced a 'Bill to Amend the Provisions for the Future Government of Ireland' on 13 February 1893. This second Home Rule Bill proposed two houses – the upper to be known as the Legislative Council, and the lower as the Legislative Assembly. The Council, to be elected for a period of eight years, was to consist of 48 members, and the franchise would be confined to owners and occupiers of properties of a rateable value of £20 or more. The Assembly was to comprise 103 members, to be elected for a five-year term by the existing House of Commons electorate. Restrictions were to be placed on certain areas, including land law and the constabulary, but the chief subject of concern to the Irish Party was the question of finances, in particular the size of the surplus that would be under the control of the Irish parliament after its imperial contribution had been extracted.

In addition to financial concerns, there was indecision on the important question of whether Irish MPs should continue to sit in the Commons after Home Rule was granted. Some Liberals saw the removal of Irish MPs from Westminster as the best reason for supporting Home Rule. Others such as Harcourt favoured the retention of Irish members, as they would still be needed to support English domestic reforms. Originally, 80 Irish MPs were to be allowed to sit in the Commons, but only when topics affecting

Ireland were being discussed. It was never clarified how this proposal would work in practice and, during the committee stage, the bill was amended so that Irish MPs would still be permanent members of the House.

Speaking for 'the Nationalist Party', just days before Gladstone introduced the second Home Rule Bill, McCarthy stated in the Commons that 'an attempt is being made to bring about a true union between Great Britain and Ireland'. Going on to discuss related matters, he looked forward to a time when 'for ever we may get rid of the bad feeling between the two peoples'.[26]

McCarthy further expressed his views on the bill in an article in the March 1893 issue of *Nineteenth Century*. Here, he outlined his reservations, ranging from the trivial ('I wish the representative chamber were not called a Legislative Assembly') to the serious ('Its financial clauses . . . are anything but satisfactory'). Despite such reservations, he clearly expected to be able to reach a compromise with the Liberals, as he predicted that the bill would pass the Commons in that session. Thereafter it would be thrown out by the Lords and, when passed again by the Commons (probably in an autumn session), the ensuing agitation would be sufficient 'to induce the House of Lords to think twice before venturing upon a second veto'.[27]

In April 1893 he spoke during the Second Reading debate on the proposed legislation, saying that

No man, no administration, no set of remedial measures, can ever win the Irish people from their desire for national self-government. That was the one reason for the right hon. Gentleman [Gladstone] bringing in his measure of Home Rule, because he saw that with nothing else would the Irish people be contented. He has reason now to believe that with such a measure the Irish people most certainly would be content.[28]

McCarthy went on to say 'frankly' that the Nationalist Party would strive to amend certain provisions when the bill went into committee, and that he 'could not possibly say that we are satisfied with the Financial Clauses of the Bill as they now stand'.[29] Notwithstanding these reservations:

> my friends and I do accept that Bill as an honest attempt at a settlement of the whole National question . . . we have one thing that we especially want, and that is the right to make our local legislation for ourselves. As I understand, this measure will give us that right subject only to those reasonable precautions and checks and guarantees which the Bill contains, and which we are perfectly willing to accept.

He went on to say that

> so far as our foresight will enable us to look into the future, we do believe that the measure when duly improved in Committee will be, for at all events our time, a final settlement of the Irish Question. We shall welcome this Bill . . . as a final settlement between Great Britain and Ireland.[30]

In addition to endeavouring to persuade British MPs and the British public that this bill was a final settlement, not an interim measure on the road to full independence, McCarthy also tried to convince Irish Unionists and Protestants that minority rights would be protected in a Home Rule Ireland. Events such as the 'blatant intervention' of the Roman Catholic hierarchy in Irish politics following the O'Shea divorce case had 'confirmed apprehensions that Protestants and unionists would be excluded from public life under home rule'.[31]

Speaking at the Committee stage, in favour of the principle of having a Second Chamber in the proposed Home Rule parliament, McCarthy said that

We know that there is in Ireland, and possibly in England, a certain fear that the interests of the minority might be overborne under possible conditions by the strength of the majority. We are also assured that to meet that possible dread or susceptibilities of that kind the most convenient form of protection for minorities would be the creation of a Second Chamber. . . we, on that account, are perfectly willing to assist in the formation of a Second Chamber.[32]

McCarthy addressed only the principle of a second chamber, admitting that 'We have nothing to do with what hereafter may be proposed as to the construction, or position, or constitution of that Second Chamber.' Continuing, he said that

we are quite willing to give so much consideration to the interests, and probably the honest and sincere alarms of the Irish minority, or some of them, we are quite willing, I say, to give so much attention and regard to that sentiment as to be willing to accept a Second Chamber as a convenient and proper institution in Ireland. . . We accept it because we believe it might be a safeguard in trying and momentous times against anything like too rapid legislation, and therefore would be a guarantee for the safety of the minority.[33]

He also addressed the issue of Ulster representation, without referring to the question of the representation of minorities in the rest of the island of Ireland:

I cannot believe that there is the slightest danger of stifling the voice of Ulster in any Constitution that can be framed for the Irish people. And I go farther, and say that there is no desire amongst the Irish Members or the Irish people that Ulster Toryism should not have its full weight, its full representation, in the National Councils.[34]

As expected, compromises were agreed between the Liberals and the Irish Party, with the latter supporting the former in moving the bill through the various legislative stages. This support continued throughout the more than 200 hours of often heated debate, spread over 82 days – a debate that at one point even erupted into physical violence. On 27 July 1893 there occurred, for about three minutes

> a common street-row on the floor of the House . . . [when] the gangway was a mass of surging, struggling humanity, wildly hitting out on every side, crushing hats, throwing one another down, and grappling with one another.[35]

'The whole thing', McCarthy wrote, on the night of the fight, 'was scandalous, shameful, sickening – an unspeakable degradation to the English Parliament',[36] and showed the passions that the subject enflamed.

One of those caught up in this melee was Colonel Edward Saunderson (a former Liberal MP for Cavan and, since 1886, the leader of the Irish Unionist Parliamentary Party), who claimed to have been hit from behind.[37] Like McCarthy, Saunderson has been a largely neglected figure of the Home Rule era. As a recent biographer has written, Saunderson, 'who for twenty years was the English face of Irish Unionism has been consigned to obscurity, the victim of shifting loyalist priorities and myth-building, and of scholarly disregard'.[38] Although McCarthy marched under a green flag, and Saunderson under an orange one, relations between the two leaders were generally cordial. They often met 'in houses of hospitable friends', and McCarthy later wrote that the 'gallant and uncompromising Orangeman . . . [was] an earnest and a devoted supporter of the cause to which he was pledged', and that Saunderson's 'professions of devotion to the Orange flag were absolutely sincere'. Saunderson would, he continued, 'risk or sacrifice his life in his own political cause'.[39]

While Saunderson led the opposition to the bill in Ireland, its main opponent in Britain was the leader of the Conservative Party, the formidable Robert Arthur Talbot Gascoyne-Cecil, third Marquess of Salisbury. Like McCarthy, Salisbury was born in 1830. There the similarities ended. Standing six foot four inches, and weighing eighteen stone five pounds in the early 1890s, Salisbury was a descendent of Robert Cecil, the first Earl of Salisbury, who had been Secretary of State to King James I at the time of the Plantation of Ulster.[40]

Availing himself of free time after the Conservatives' defeat in the 1892 general election, the third Marquess had published in the *National Review* a long constitutional justification for his opposition to any Home Rule legislation, but it has been claimed that Salisbury's 'true argument was far removed from theories of constitutional practice'. Put simply, he 'meant to stand by the Loyalists whom his ancestor had planted in Ulster'.[41] Objecting to the very concept of Home Rule for Ireland, Salisbury protested that, 'We are to cut our country in two and, in the smaller portion, we are to abandon a minority of our own blood and religion to the power of their ancient enemies, in spite of their bitter protest against their debasing and ruinous servitude to which we propose to leave them.'[42] To these arguments he later added concerns that the passing of Home Rule legislation would have negative consequences for the reputation of the British Empire (especially for British rule in India); and that a neutral or hostile Ireland would threaten Britain's supply of food in time of war.[43]

In general, Tory opposition to Home Rule was based on – sometimes contradictory – beliefs that the Irish did not constitute a separate people; were unfit or at least unready for extensive powers of self-government; were likely to ill-treat the Protestant minority; and would eventually push for full separation. The last, it was argued, would damage the security of Great Britain, as it would create a possibly hostile neighbour just off Britain's western shore. It was also feared that certain colonial subjects, and some less-than-friendly foreign powers, would consider that Britain would henceforth neither defend its own territory nor support its friends.[44]

On 1 September 1893 McCarthy, opening the last night's debate on the third reading of the Home Rule Bill, tried to address some of these Conservative and Unionist fears when he declared that

> speaking for the Irish Party, we are perfectly willing to accept it . . . [as] a final settlement, because it will enable us to work in the most thorough cordiality with the people of Great Britain.[45]

At the end of that night's proceedings, the second Home Rule Bill passed the Commons by 301 votes to 267.

Despite this success, McCarthy's efforts – and those of the Liberals – to address the concerns of those opposed to Home Rule for Ireland were apparently all in vain. Gladstone, the Irish Nationalist's champion in the Commons was, according to McCarthy, 'the first great English statesmen who ever risked power and popularity for the sake of doing justice to Ireland'.[46] Gladstone's problem was that, in the House of Commons, he had a small majority. Salisbury, on the other hand, the Irish Unionists' champion, had an unassailable one in the House of Lords. Saunderson and his fellow Irish squires had 'a remarkable influence over sections of the Conservative leadership throughout the 1890s, and in particular over Lord Salisbury'.[47] On 8 September 1893, Salisbury's influence in the Lords was clearly demonstrated when the second Home Rule Bill was rejected in that House by 419 votes to 41.

In view of this defeat, obvious questions must be considered. Did McCarthy waste his life in pursuit of an impossible dream?

And did Gladstone similarly waste the years 1886–93 in search of a crowning glory to his career, only to end in ignominious failure? R. C. K. Ensor writes of Gladstone, 'All his long effort since 1886 might seem fruitless. Yet we can now see that, whether for good or evil, it was not.' Ensor continues:

> The Home Rule Bill of 1886 had been only a flash in the pan. The commons had rejected its bare principles; its details were not reached. Had it lacked a sequel for nineteen years, there might never have been one. But the bill of 1893 went through all stages in the elected house. It emerged a complete measure which, but for the veto of the house of lords, would have come into force. It was almost bound to be revived if and when a majority of the nation took the view that the lords used their veto unfairly.[48]

Ensor's assessment of Gladstone might also be applied to McCarthy. By maintaining both the unity of the Irish Party and the Liberal alliance, McCarthy helped to ensure the passage of the Home Rule Bill through the Commons, thereby greatly strengthening the Irish parliamentary tradition. In the fluid political situation after the Irish Party split of 1890, and during the heated political climate of 1892–3, these were major achievements.

At the beginning of March 1894, the 84-year-old Gladstone at last resigned from his positions as Prime Minister and leader of the Liberal Party, and was replaced in both roles by his Foreign Secretary, the Earl of Rosebery. Rosebery's situation was quite similar to that of McCarthy. Both had replaced men of heroic stature (Gladstone and Parnell), and both were to have their positions undermined by former equals, who were now their subordinates. Harcourt, very disappointed by his failure to achieve the premiership, resolved to have nothing but official relations with Rosebery. The new Prime Minister, for his part, was sometimes less than friendly towards his cabinet colleagues. When, for example, Home Secretary Asquith suggested that Morley, although difficult to manage, was at least a perfect gentleman, Rosebery replied, 'I am not sure whether a perfect lady would not best describe him.'[49] A number of factors, including incessant cabinet quarrels, meant that Rosebery's premiership turned out to be neither long nor enjoyable, and in June 1895 he used an unexpected defeat (on a vote on the Army Estimates) as an excuse to relinquish office. He was replaced by Salisbury. A general election followed in July.

While the Liberals suffered a major defeat in this 1895 election – in McCarthy's mid-election phrase, they were routed 'horse, foot and artillery'[50] – the Irish Party appeared to have a satisfactory result. In 1892 the party had won 72 seats, and in 1895 they had 70 MPs elected. In addition, 61 Irish seats were uncontested this time, compared to only 21 three years earlier. This was a major financial saving for the party. These facts, however, conceal the real picture. The 1895 general election was a bitterly fought contest, not between parties, but within the Irish Party itself, and 'the price paid for this public exhibition of the dissension inside the [party] . . . ranks was a heavy one'.[51] As this dissension occurred during McCarthy's leadership and was, indeed, a major irritant throughout it, this is an appropriate place to assess McCarthy's performance as party leader.

Comparisons with Parnell serve little useful purpose. In the past 200 years, figures such as O'Connell, Parnell and de Valera have stood head-and-shoulders above their contemporaries, but a party leader can still give a very credible performance, even if he does not dominate his age. Accepting this, how should McCarthy be judged?

For almost five years, through patient and conciliatory chairmanship, he maintained both the unity of the party and the Liberal alliance. Considering the circumstances in which the leadership was thrust upon him, these were significant achievements. When the Irish Party first elected him as sessional chairman in December 1890, it was also decided to elect an eight-man committee to exercise joint authority with the chairman. The positive effect of this decision was that henceforth all power was not concentrated in one man; the negative effect was that one man's decisiveness was replaced by a committee's indecisiveness.

McCarthy was well aware of the handicap the committee system imposed upon him, and he knew that 'the very basis of my leadership is that there should be no dictatorship'.[52] Ambitious men such as Healy and Dillon, once freed from Parnell's control, now sought to direct party policy. The shared leadership, a natural reaction to Parnell's autocratic *modus operandi*, therefore almost guaranteed that party indiscipline would be a major feature of McCarthy's chairmanship.

McCarthy's achievement in maintaining party unity has not always been recognised. In his biography of John Dillon, for example, F. S. L. Lyons writes that McCarthy 'was totally incapable of standing up to Healy, or for that matter to Dillon. He was ageing, in poor health and trying by his writing to discharge a mountain of debts.'[53] This is a fair assessment in terms of the age, health, and debt issues, but not so the allegation that McCarthy was incapable of standing up to other members of the party.

The achievement of Home Rule was McCarthy's main goal: 'People would be unable to understand how much this National Cause has been the religion of my life.'[54] He believed that in order to achieve Home Rule it was essential for the unity of the Irish Party to be maintained. One of the strengths of the party both in Ireland and at Westminster, especially in the period from the introduction of the pledge in 1885 to the split in 1890, was its unity. Whenever this unity was weakened, its power in parliament was concomitantly reduced. McCarthy was therefore determined not to allow another schism to occur.

In such circumstances, the problem was not that McCarthy was incapable of standing up to Healy and Dillon. In 1891 Dillon declined even to consider accepting the position of chairman, simply because of the difficulties involved.[55] McCarthy had not sought, but neither had he shirked, the demands of the chairmanship. As he proved on a number of occasions, he was well capable of taking a stand when necessary. He had shown this early on when, in the face of Parnell's threatened resignation over the 1881 land bill, he had voted against Parnell's policy of abstention on the second reading.[56] He showed it again when he led his colleagues out of Committee Room 15 in December 1890. McCarthy was aware that, were he to tackle head-on the issue of indiscipline, he would create a crisis that would not only further divide the party, but would also seriously lessen the chances of achieving Home Rule. His policy of conciliation rather than confrontation should not therefore be seen as a sign of weakness, but rather as evidence of political maturity and realism.

McCarthy's leadership should also be viewed in a wider context. Both Parnell and Gladstone dominated their parties – the former for a decade, the latter for considerably longer. Both parties experienced a similar fate when these political giants left the stage. After their departures, their respective parties were riven by internal strife, with cabals jostling for position. The fact that McCarthy remained as chairman for over five years is testimony to the steeliness of his character and to the high regard in which he was held by his colleagues.

After Parnell's forced departure, the Irish Party had three leaders in ten years: McCarthy (1890–6), Dillon (1896–9), and Redmond, who was elected leader of a reunited Irish Party in February 1900. During these years, the Liberals suffered a similar period of discontinuity. Gladstone retired in March 1894, to be succeeded by Rosebery (1894–6), Harcourt (1896–8), and Sir

Henry Campbell-Bannerman (1899–1908). McCarthy's more
than five-year period as leader was significantly longer than the
terms served by Rosebery, Dillon or Harcourt. At a time when
these leaders were involved in games of political musical chairs, the
Conservatives under Salisbury (from 1885 to 1902), and the
Unionists under Saunderson (from 1886 to 1906) each had one
leader only during the turbulent 1890s.

A contemporary recalled McCarthy as a

> modest and agreeable man of letters, courtly after the older manner,
> soft in step and gentle in voice, with only a slight and agreeable trace of
> brogue. . . [who] was in his way as indomitable an Irish Nationalist as
> any of those unhappy fellow-countrymen whose death on the scaffold
> it was his mournful duty as a historian to chronicle.[57]

It was this indomitable nature that allowed him to lead the Irish
Party through such a politically volatile period.

McCarthy's policy of positive conciliation (as opposed to self-
defeating confrontation) was recognised by his party colleague,
William O'Brien. In his *Recollections*, O'Brien wrote that McCarthy's
'sweetness of nature did not in the least lessen his firmness upon
the proper occasion'. As an example, O'Brien recalled that in 1893,
when Healy had threatened to secede from the party with nineteen
supporters if McCarthy (as chairman) voted against Healy at a
forthcoming meeting, McCarthy 'gently stroking his beard' defused
the situation by replying, 'That would be very unfortunate – for
the nineteen. Time is up for our meeting. Tim, let us have a glass of
grog.' On another occasion, McCarthy diplomatically 'threw oil
upon the rising waters of Party strife' and settled a conflict between
O'Brien and Healy.[58] This policy of non-confrontation maintained
the unity of the party and facilitated the passing of a Home Rule
Bill by the Commons – something even Parnell had been unable to

accomplish. For these achievements, McCarthy's leadership should be considered a period of significant (albeit limited) success.

During McCarthy's time as chairman, despite the outward unity of the party, a number of serious internal disputes occurred, some of which became public and seriously damaged the party's reputation and standing. These disputes should be briefly considered, as their resolution – or lack thereof – again show McCarthy's preference for conciliation rather than confrontation.

The first major source of conflict within the party concerned the merger of the *National Press* with the *Freeman's Journal*. Even after the party had launched the *National Press* in March 1891, McCarthy and his senior colleagues continued in their attempts to separate the *Freeman* from the Parnellite camp. In September 1891 they succeeded, and it was decided that the two newspapers should be amalgamated, under the title of the more commercially successful *Freeman's Journal*. This merger was strenuously but unsuccessfully opposed by Healy, the *National Press*'s editor, who had been using his editorial position as a personal power base.

The initial dispute over the merger, and the subsequent disagreement over the new board of directors of the amalgamated *Freeman*, threatened to split the party again, during the lead-up to the 1892 general election, and later nearly jeopardised the passage of the 1893 Home Rule Bill. Writing shortly before the election about the dispute, McCarthy told Praed that 'there is so much sensitiveness, so much jealousy, so much rancour, so much passion, so much *hysteria* – women are not the only hysterical creatures in this world'.[59] In June 1893, during the Home Rule debate, the internal conflict continued and McCarthy confessed to being 'well-nigh sick of it all. I have ruined health and literary work for this!'[60] There was fortunately a successful mediation of the dispute, which had been largely hidden from public view and consequently had little detrimental impact on the party's public standing. Subsequent disputes would, however, become increasingly public, and would progressively erode confidence in the party.

Three of these subsequent disputes, each calling into question McCarthy's key policy of alliance with the Liberals, further strained the party's unity in 1894–5. These concerned: first, Rosebery's commitment to Home Rule; second, the acceptance of financial support from senior Liberal Party figures; and third, the alleged 'sale' of four Ulster parliamentary seats to the Liberal Party. Each of these incidents could have split the party but, through patient negotiations, McCarthy managed to maintain both the Liberal alliance and at least the outward unity of the party.

In March 1894, a week after he became Prime Minister, Rosebery caused consternation in the Irish Party by seeming to admit an English veto over the question of Irish Home Rule. Five days later he gave an explanation of his policy and, although this was acceptable to the majority of the Irish Party, McCarthy still had what he considered to be the busiest week of his political career. Private meetings and marathon party sessions followed Rosebery's veto announcement, with the party 'torn by internal dissensions', as it debated its policy towards Rosebery's government, and 'all the while, some of us have to keep up a good appearance in the more or less futile hope of concealing from the world the true and ominous story of our troubles'.[61] While the majority of the party was prepared to remain true to the Liberal alliance – as Home Rule could be gained only with Liberal support – the Healyites adopted an almost Parnellite policy of independent opposition. Having survived the immediate crisis, in April 1894 McCarthy tried to heal divisions with a ninety-minute speech to the party on the need to get 'rid of dissensions'.[62] Despite the disagreements over policy, in the end the party did not split on the issue.

The next dispute followed McCarthy's decision in August 1894 to accept financial donations to the Irish Party from senior

Liberals. Earlier that month an appeal for funds had been launched
in England, and McCarthy was surprised to receive two £100
cheques in response to this appeal – one from Lord Tweedmouth,
a member of Rosebery's cabinet, and the other from Gladstone.
McCarthy gratefully accepted these contributions and had them
acknowledged, as was customary, in the *Freeman's Journal*. His
decision to accept the donations led to a series of attacks on him
and on the policy of the Liberal alliance. In reply to this criticism, McCarthy stated in a published telegram that, 'It would be
stupid rudeness to refuse the subscriptions.' He also took 'entire
responsibility for accepting subscriptions and publishing [the
donors'] names'.[63]

McCarthy considered the matter to 'be really a tornado in a tea-
pot', and disagreed that the acceptance of the cheques constituted
a surrender of the independence of the Irish Party to the Liberals,
as was publicly claimed by the Healyites. He accepted, however,
that 'the controversy rages and has become a scandal'.[64] Under
pressure, a compromise was reached, whereby all funds received
from Englishmen were returned to their donors – with one
exception. At McCarthy's insistence, Gladstone's donation was
retained. This solution somewhat restored public confidence in
the party, although support for McCarthy's prized Liberal alliance
was damaged by the incident.

As well as his detractors, McCarthy had his supporters. Edward
Blake, for instance, fund-raising for the party in America, loyally
tried to minimise the damage to the cause in general, and to
McCarthy in particular. 'It would', Blake wrote, 'be a poor return
for his [McCarthy's] services and sacrifices to his country, that his
friends should think for a moment of any other line of conduct.'[65]

The general election of 1895 provided the background to the
third major Liberal Party related controversy of McCarthy's
chairmanship. Salisbury dissolved parliament in June, and the

elections took place in July. With the Irish Party fairly evenly divided between the supporters of McCarthy and Healy, it was essential for each side to control the selection of candidates for the election. On 24 June, a party meeting decided that the management of the election campaign should be entrusted to McCarthy and the party's executive committee. Aware that his supporters were in a minority on that committee, Healy launched a public campaign against his party colleagues.

At Healy-dominated meetings of the Irish National Federation's executive committee in early July, resolutions were passed condemning the placing of the party's committee in charge of the election campaign, and challenging the authority of the party's committee to summon conventions of delegates. McCarthy published his response in the *Freeman's Journal* on 4 July. Although flexible on minor matters of concern to the Federation, he was firm in his refusal to tolerate its interference in party affairs. He wrote that, 'The executive of the National Federation was elected for the internal management of the Federation, and the Irish Party cannot recognise any right in such a body to control or overrule the work of the party.'[66] Four days later, the party suffered the worst blow to its internal unity since the Parnell split, and a crippling blow to its reputation, from an event that became known as the 'Omagh scandal'.

On 8 July the party's County Tyrone selection convention was held in Omagh and, according to the newspapers, Healy alleged at the convention that the party had previously written to the Liberals and agreed to 'sell' them four Ulster seats – North and South Tyrone, and North and South Londonderry – for an annual payment. Healy disputed the newspaper reports, but refused to clarify what exactly he had said at the meeting. Made as it was during an election campaign, the allegation was a public relations disaster for the party.

There was, in fact, no such agreement. The relevant correspondence shows that the Irish Party had informed the Liberal Home Rulers – by now a rare species – 'that if the work of registration was to be carried on in Tyrone and Londonderry . . . it would have to be paid for by the Liberal Home Rulers with the logical corollary that the seats would be fought at the general election as Liberal Home Rule seats'.[67] McCarthy denounced the allegations as 'baseless charges', and later accused Healy of 'disloyalty to the party'.[68] He refused, however, to release the correspondence, presumably because it was confidential, and also because it was 'a humiliating confession of poverty and weakness'.[69]

In the general election, McCarthy was returned unopposed for North Longford on 16 July,[70] and on 13 August was re-elected sessional chairman of the party, for the last time. Three days later, a party motion approving his actions and those of the committee (in connection with the four Ulster seats), but avoiding any condemnation of Healy, was narrowly passed by 33 votes to 26. With this vote, the party ended its formal discussion of the 'Omagh scandal'. The close vote showed the strength of Healy's following, and confirmed the need for McCarthy's non-confrontational policy. In such an evenly balanced situation, a policy of confrontation would have split the party in two. But Healy was soon to make a tactical mistake that would considerably weaken his position.

In late August 1895 a parliamentary vacancy occurred in South Kerry, and Healy organised a convention that, with clerical backing, nominated William Martin Murphy (a former financial supporter of his *National Press*) as a candidate for the by-election.[71] In opposition to Murphy, the Irish Party officially nominated a London Irishman, T. J. Farrell. The two candidates, purportedly from the same party, then carried their conflict to the hustings. On 1 September McCarthy, no longer able to play down internal party differences, issued a manifesto claiming that Murphy's nomination brought 'the whole people of Ireland face to face with a momentous issue'. 'The forces of revolt,' he wrote, 'against which my colleagues who are loyal to the party pledge, and myself, have been fighting for three years, have chosen a moment for forcing the decision between unity and disruption.'[72] On this occasion, McCarthy's forces of unity won.

South Kerry was important for three reasons. First, there was an open split on the hustings, and so the policies of both sides were publicly debated and assessed. Second, it resulted in a comfortable win for McCarthy's side (by 1,209 votes for Farrell to 474 for Murphy), which showed that his preference for an independent party, in close alliance with the Liberals, still commanded majority support. Third, it presented an opportunity to weaken Healy. While he still commanded too much support to be expelled from the party, over a period of eight days in November 1895 Healy was removed from the executive of the Irish National League of Great Britain, the council of the Federation, and the committee of the party. Although this was not the end for Healy, it did mean that his influence was severely curtailed. (He would eventually be expelled from the party in 1900.) It was, however, the end for McCarthy. In February 1896 he resigned his chairmanship.

As early as 1891, McCarthy had wanted to resign as chairman. Even the Liberals were well aware of his intentions. On 21 January 1891 Earl Granville wrote to Gladstone that McCarthy was anxious to vacate the leadership, 'as it prevents him earning his bread by writing'.[73] Having reluctantly accepted the post, McCarthy quickly tried to relinquish it. In early February 1891, with the collapse of the Boulogne negotiations, with Parnell determined to fight on, and with Dillon and O'Brien soon to be lodged in Galway jail, McCarthy accepted that it was 'impossible for me to get out of the leadership all at once as I had some hope of being able to do'. His mind was, however, 'absolutely made up to get out of the position the first moment that I can'.[74]

In the spring of 1891 he hoped for another opportunity to relinquish the post. The negotiations to detach the *Freeman's Journal* from Parnell's camp were going well, and McCarthy optimistically believed that, if successful, 'the crisis will be over',[75] thereby allowing him 'to withdraw with honour from the leadership and leave a united party'.[76] In order to maintain party unity, he found it necessary to remain as chairman for almost a further five years. No unanimous replacement was available, and there was a natural reluctance to take on the unenviable role of chairman. Dillon, a likely successor, lacked enthusiasm for the post. 'Under present conditions', he wrote in July 1891, he considered 'the chairmanship . . . a position of hideous and frightful responsibility'.[77] McCarthy meanwhile continued to sacrifice his health and financial position, and reluctantly continued to bear the 'hideous and frightful responsibility' involved.

Health was a constant source of concern, and in March 1891 McCarthy's doctor diagnosed nervous exhaustion. When his colleagues set off for the by-election campaign in North Sligo, McCarthy also departed, 'not to Sligo, but to the Riviera'.[78] There he joined Praed, who later recalled that he was 'of much weaker health and shattered nerves'.[79] Physical exhaustion and an attack of influenza in mid-May 1891 kept him away from the Commons for two months. A year later, an electioneering trip to Ireland brought on a cold and rheumatism, and again led to confinement. On this occasion he admitted to Praed that he 'had so much stress of political work of late' that he took some relief from 'being absolutely prevented from going to any meeting, committee, debate or division!'[80]

Ill health in fact plagued McCarthy's leadership. In late February 1893, after the introduction of the Home Rule Bill, he was housebound by his doctor; and in August 1894 he wrote to Praed that he was 'in a broken-down condition'. He said that he had received an urgent request from his colleagues to come to Ireland but 'they might as well ask me to travel to the Ural Mountains just now as to travel to Dublin'.[81]

His finances were also a cause of much concern, as a result of the Irish Exhibition debacle. Physically and financially exhausted, his personal goal was a quiet literary life in England or America, but political demands made this impossible. Particularly during the period after the Liberals were returned to office in 1892, he became increasingly involved in committee, party and public meetings.

In December 1892 he decided temporarily to stop writing late leaders for the *Daily News*, and instead to write articles from home. This meant a drop in income, but he was sixty-two and, in view of the heavy demands of political negotiations, had to jettison the additional burden of 'writing a late leading article in winter and . . . driving home at about three o'clock [in the morning] amid storm and sleet and rain'.[82] In February 1893 political commitments required him to take a complete break from writing for the *News*. Thus, despite his personal financial problems, he temporarily gave up his most regular source of income. In a period when MPs were not paid a salary, he was seriously risking his health and finances for the cause of Home Rule.

The failure to enact the second Home Rule Bill did not mean that McCarthy had sufficient time for remunerative writing, and in early 1895 he continued to produce not very lucrative 'pot-boilers' – leading articles for the *Daily News* and contributions to American magazines. He had, however, to postpone work on his histories. These took too long to write and, while the return might have been good, it was also very slow. Like his party, he was in urgent need of funds.

The combined physical and financial strain, allied to the internal party difficulties, contributed to his growing disenchantment with political life. He wrote to Praed in November 1894 that, 'I grow to dislike political work more and more.'[83] In February 1895 he confessed to having two nightmares – 'the bitter weather and the House of Commons'.[84] Gone were the relaxed days of the 1880s, when he could enjoy pranks at social evenings, and misleading political gossip columnists.[85]

McCarthy reluctantly agreed to stand again at the July 1895 general election. He was by now 'utterly weary' of politics and longed to be free of 'the insufferable drudgery of public life'. It was feared, however, that his resignation on the eve of a general election, and at a time of great discord within the party, would have a negative impact on both it and the Liberals at the forthcoming election. There were also concerns regarding the likely effects of an Irish Party leadership contest at that time. McCarthy therefore consented to go forward for re-election 'on the express understanding with my colleagues that I am to be perfectly free . . . to resign my seat at any time I may think fit'.[86]

On 21 December 1895 Dillon wrote to O'Brien that McCarthy was 'fixed in the resolve that he must go'.[87] According to Dillon, McCarthy wanted to announce his resignation in mid-January 1896.[88] He was, however, persuaded to delay the announcement until the eve of the new session of parliament, in order to avoid internal party intrigue. A leak of his intention meant that no purpose was served by further delay, and in early February 1896 he issued his formal farewell address – some ten weeks after his 65th birthday.

McCarthy's first choice as successor was Thomas Sexton, but Sexton would not accept the post. McCarthy considered that the next best option was 'to use our majority and elect John Dillon', as he considered the latter to be 'absolutely single-minded and devoted to the national cause'. Furthermore, 'He has a home in Ireland, and he has not to make a living.'[89] In view of McCarthy's own financial circumstances, the last point was understandably important.

McCarthy made his last major contribution to the Irish Party when he proposed Dillon as chairman. Elected on 18 February 1896 – by the surprisingly large margin of 38 votes to 21 – Dillon began his period as chairman, which was to last until February 1899. With Dillon's election, McCarthy's active parliamentary career ended.

* * *

Despite poor health at the time of his resignation, McCarthy lived another sixteen years. He took no further significant part in politics, and whatever energy he did possess he now devoted to literary pursuits. He finished a life of Pope Leo XIII (for a series on 'Public Men of To-Day'), and wrote a life of Gladstone, which he considered to be merely another pot-boiler, for an American publisher. 'But', he lamented, 'if the garrison is to hold out there must be something in the pot to boil.'[90] He also wrote the fifth volume of his *A History of Our Own Times*, which was rushed out in 1897 for Queen Victoria's Diamond Jubilee Year. The strain of this forced activity nearly killed him.

In the late spring of 1897, worn out by overwork and anxiety, his health broke down and he was given the Last Rites of the Roman Catholic Church. He survived, but never fully recovered. In July 1897 he and his daughter, Charlotte, who devoted herself to looking after him, moved to Westgate-on-Sea in Kent, where he was to spend most of the rest of his life and where he continued to write. 'I shall go on writing books', he informed Praed, 'because I have to write them, and that is all.'[91] His later works included his two-volume *Reminiscences*, published in 1899.

As his sight failed, he had to dictate his books (and later his correspondence) to a secretary. Of his many infirmities, he considered 'the increasing defects of eyesight . . . the most depressing'.[92] This deterioration of sight brought on feelings of 'melancholy' that were to persist for the rest of his life, which he now considered 'mere retrospect'. He nevertheless remained productive. The two concluding volumes of his history of the Georges – now entitled *A History of the Four Georges and of William IV* – appeared in 1901 (with his son, Justin Huntly, named as co-author). His novel, *Mononia: A Love Story of 'Forty-Eight'*, was published the same year. He saw it as 'a sort of bequest to the dear, old Cause'.[93] A book on the reign of Queen Anne followed soon after, and he continued to contribute a monthly letter to the New York *Independent*, and wrote occasional articles for the *Daily News*.

In late 1902 the Conservative Prime Minister, Arthur Balfour, recommended McCarthy for a Civil List pension of £250 a year for services to literature. It was a generous gesture by a political opponent, and was gratefully accepted. (McCarthy would later play a minor role in the campaign that in 1910 led to W. B. Yeats being awarded a Civil List pension of £150 per annum.[94]) Despite his pension, McCarthy did not cease to dictate books. His autobiography, *The Story of an Irishman*, and the two concluding volumes of his *A History of Our Own Times*, ending with the accession of King Edward VII in 1901, followed in due course. His last work, *Irish Recollections*, was published in 1911. In the late summer of that year he grew noticeably weaker, his sight further deteriorated, and his memory began to fail.

On 11 April 1912 Herbert Henry Asquith introduced the third Home Rule Bill into the Commons. It now fell to former Parnellite John Redmond, as Irish Party chairman, to support a Liberal

Prime Minister while the latter steered a Home Rule Bill through the Houses of Parliament. It is not known whether McCarthy was aware of this development. Twelve days after Asquith introduced the bill, on 23 April 1912 McCarthy again received the Last Rites of his Church. He died shortly before eight o'clock the following evening. He was 81 years old. Despite suggestions that his remains be returned to Ireland, he was buried beside his wife, Charlotte, in Highgate Cemetery, London. His personal estate was valued at £197.

Conclusion

Justin McCarthy was a well-respected and popular figure. He was also a fluent writer who enjoyed a distinguished career as a journalist, editor, novelist and historian. He was ambitious and talented, and could easily have made a comfortable living as a writer in Ireland, England or America. He was welcomed into London society homes, and seemed assured of a rewarding and profitable literary career.

McCarthy, however, was also patriotic. Shortly after he was elected to parliament, he became involved in the Irish Party's campaign of obstruction, with a concomitantly negative (albeit temporary) effect on both his popularity and his income. With the ending of obstruction, his integrity and talent made him a respected figure in the House of Commons, and it is as a politician, first as party vice-chairman and later as chairman, that he is judged here.

In United Kingdom politics from the mid-1880s, Gladstone and Salisbury were larger-than-life, rival leaders. In the smaller pond of Irish politics at that time, Parnell had no rival, inside or outside his party. McCarthy, as party vice-chairman, was therefore understandably overshadowed by him. The role of vice-chairman is a notoriously difficult one to play. McCarthy, who concentrated his activities on behind-the-scenes negotiations on Parnell's behalf, played it loyally and competently. Whether during the Kilmainham negotiations of 1882 or the Carnarvon discussions of 1885, McCarthy proved to be a skilful political negotiator who was trusted by both the Liberals and the Conservatives. He was, further-more, a moderating force within the Irish Party, and an able deputy at party meetings during Parnell's absences. For many reasons, therefore, Parnell was justifiably concerned when McCarthy proposed to retire from politics in 1887.

McCarthy had no wish to replace Parnell as party leader. After the divorce court decision, he endeavoured to arrange the contin-uation of Parnell's chairmanship, but the publication of Gladstone's letter to Morley presented the party with a stark choice – Parnell or expected Home Rule. In these tense circumstances McCarthy, who believed in the cause over the individual, successfully under-took the difficult task of detaching the majority of the party from Parnell (without appearing to be acting at Gladstone's behest), while maintaining the crucial Liberal alliance.

McCarthy's chairmanship was personally not a happy period and, although reluctant to retain the post, he did so for five difficult years. Parnell had clung on to the position of party chairman in November–December 1890 for purely personal gain, even though it was plainly not in the interests of the Home Rule cause that he do so. The fact that McCarthy, on the other hand, stayed on in an unwelcome and onerous post, despite his physical and financial problems, bears testimony to his unselfish patriotism. (It might be noted that in 1891 a younger, fitter, and wealthier John Dillon would not accept the leadership, owing to the difficulties involved; and in 1896 Thomas Sexton also declined to lead the party.)

McCarthy's greatest achievements as chairman were the main-tenance of the unity of the Irish Party, and the consequent passing by the Commons of the second Home Rule Bill. He also maintained the Liberal alliance, despite the external challenges of Parnell and John Redmond, and the internal challenges of Healy. McCarthy was a realist who accepted that only with the support of the Liberal Party would any degree of Home Rule be granted to Ireland. Once

Gladstone finally decided to support Home Rule, the Irish Party became in effect the prisoner of the Liberals. Salisbury, who 'felt a cold contempt'[1] for the forces of Irish Nationalism, had no intention of repeating the 1885 Conservative flirtation with the Irish Party. McCarthy therefore had to eschew the easy but self-defeating policy of opposition, in favour of the more-demanding but ultimately also more-rewarding Liberal alliance. An alternative to that policy would be attempted on Easter Monday 1916.

As party chairman, McCarthy practised a policy of conciliation rather than confrontation – with both the Liberals and the Healyites. With the Liberals, it resulted in the second Home Rule Bill being passed by the Commons; with the Healyites, it maintained party unity, without which the Liberal alliance would not have continued. In the charged atmosphere of the post-Parnell period, it was essential that democratic politics achieve even this limited degree of success. Otherwise, different forces, less democratic in aims and methods, would have filled the void.

McCarthy has been portrayed by some as a weak individual,[2] but not all held this view. George W. E. Russell, MP for North Bedfordshire when the second Home Rule Bill was going through the Commons, while admitting that 'he [McCarthy] and I did not always agree in politics',[3] later wrote of McCarthy that

> Small in stature, delicate in constitution, pacific in temperament, he suddenly proved himself equal to exertions and endurances of which one would have judged him physically incapable. His natural fluency became eloquence; . . . His prudence in counsel, his anxiety to avoid needless offence, and his dignified demeanour, were exactly the qualities which a parliamentary leader requires; and it was observed that 'his qualities and even his defects marked him out as the easiest man for his colleagues to rally round in the place of their deposed dictator.'[4]

In a much-quoted phrase, T. P. O'Connor once said that, 'One could almost wish Justin McCarthy had been hanged, if it were only to show how a quiet man could die for Ireland.'[5] William O'Brien also wrote about McCarthy's calmness 'in hours of crisis':

> Having a keen sense of humour, he would be the last to repeat for himself the somewhat transpontine boast: *Si fractus illabatur orbis, Impavidum me ferient ruinae*; but of no man could it be with more certainty said that, if the ruins of a falling world were tumbling around him, [those who had seen him] would find him not merely unafraid, but cheerful.[6]

These qualities of leadership did not go unobserved by Parnell, who had known McCarthy since 1876, and had chosen him as his deputy in 1880. McCarthy was not one of those MPs who had been brought into parliament from 1885 on, by which time 'a rigorously policed organisational hierarchy was in place, responsible largely to Parnell himself',[7] to provide voting fodder for an autocratic leader then at the zenith of his power. Already a figure of considerable standing long before he met Parnell, McCarthy did not owe his position as an MP to the latter.

Parnell was well aware of McCarthy's quiet self-confidence. During a conversation in Boulogne, O'Brien was attempting to impress upon Parnell that McCarthy, although proving difficult, had no wish to wound him. The recently deposed 'Uncrowned King of Ireland' replied: 'My dear O'Brien, you don't know that old gentleman when he wields his umbrella.'[8]

Parnell had reason to know.

Notes

Introduction

1 The political party of which McCarthy was a member was known variously as the Home Rule Party, the Nationalist Party, the Irish Parliamentary Party, and the Irish Party. McCarthy tended to refer to it by the last name, and that is the version most commonly used in this book. In 1890 McCarthy was elected leader of the party to replace Charles Stewart Parnell, after the O'Shea divorce controversy. Those MPs who supported Parnell rapidly declined in number – at the 1892 general election they were reduced to a mere rump of nine. While it appears reasonable to refer to this group as the 'Parnellites', this author does not consider it reasonable to refer to the more than 70 MPs led by McCarthy, after that election, as the 'Anti-Parnellites', and so that term is not used in this book. As McCarthy had the backing of the majority of his parliamentary colleagues, he claimed, with reason, that he led *the* Irish Party.

2 *Dictionary of National Biography, 1912–1921* (London, 1927), p. 351.

Chapter 1: *The Making of an Irish Nationalist*

1 Colm Kerrigan, *Father Mathew and the Irish Temperance Movement, 1838–1849* (Cork, 1992), p. 73.

2 Justin McCarthy, *The Story of an Irishman* (London, 1904), p. 13.

3 Ibid., p. 3.

4 E. T. Raymond, *Portraits of the Nineties* (London, 1921), p. 243.

5 McCarthy, *Irishman*, p. 62.

6 Justin McCarthy, *Reminiscences* (2nd edn, 2 vols, London, 1899), I, p. 328.

7 Ibid., p. 426.

8 McCarthy, *Irishman*, p. 78.

Chapter 2: *The Development of a Liberal Propagandist*

1   *Northern Daily Times*, 24 Sept. 1853.
2   H. C. G. Matthew (ed.), *The Gladstone Diaries*, V: *1855–1860* (Oxford, 1978), p. 85 (12 Nov. 1855).
3   BL, W. E. Gladstone Papers, Add. MS. 44384, f. 222: McCarthy to Gladstone, 13 Nov. 1855.
4   Ibid., f. 224: McCarthy to Gladstone, 15 Nov. 1855.
5   NLI, Justin McCarthy Papers, MS 3679 (Diary), 8 Feb. 1857.
6   Asa Briggs, *Victorian People: A Reassessment of Persons and Themes, 1851–67* (Harmondsworth, 1965), p. 205.
7   *Westminster and Foreign Quarterly Review*, new series, XIX (Apr. 1861), pp. 363–80 ('Voltaire's Romances and Their Morals').
8   McCarthy, *Reminiscences*, I, p. 32.
9   Ibid., p. 37.
10 Ibid., p. 38.
11 McCarthy, *Irishman*, p. 131.
12 McCarthy, *Reminiscences*, I, p. 182.
13 Jonathan Steinberg, *Bismarck: A Life* (Oxford, 2011), p. 170.
14 McCarthy, *Reminiscences*, I, p. 183.
15 McCarthy would, of course, later become very well acquainted with John Blake Dillon's son, John Dillon.
16 McCarthy Papers, MS 3689 (Diary), 1867.
17 Ibid., 15 Dec. 1867.
18 McCarthy, *Reminiscences*, I, p. 81.
19 R. V. Comerford, 'Gladstone's first Irish enterprise, 1864–70', in W. E. Vaughan (ed.), *A New History of Ireland. V. Ireland Under the Union, I, 1801–70* (Oxford, 1989), p. 439.
20 McCarthy, *Reminiscences*, I, pp. 81–2.
21 Bright to McCarthy, 8 Nov. 1867, quoted in ibid., p. 100.
22 Alan J. Lee, *The Origins of the Popular Press in England, 1855–1914* (London, 1976), p. 108.
23 McCarthy Papers, MS 3686 (Diary), 7 Feb. 1864.
24 Ibid., 6 Mar. 1864.
25 McCarthy, *Reminiscences*, I, p. 283.
26 McCarthy, *Irishman*, p. 109.
27 McCarthy Papers, MS 3691 (Diary), 1871; Fort Wayne (Ind.) *Sentinel*, 12 Dec. 1870, quoted on flyer announcing McCarthy's lecture on 21 December 1870, slipped into his 1871 diary.

28 While McCarthy was on his lecture tour, Charlotte made her own entries in her husband's diaries. See McCarthy Papers, MS 3690 (Diary), 1870 and MS 3691 (Diary), 1871.

29 McCarthy Papers, MS 3691 (Diary), 13 Jan. 1871.

30 Ibid., 9 Feb. 1871.

31 Lee, *Origins of the Popular Press*, p. 164.

32 T. P. O'Connor, *Memoirs of an Old Parliamentarian* (2 vols, London, 1929), II, p. 69.

33 Ibid.

34 Ibid., p. 70.

35 A. M. Sullivan, *New Ireland* (16th edn, London, 1882), p. 344.

36 McCarthy, *Reminiscences*, II, p. 99.

37 Ibid., p. 91.

38 Ibid., I, p. 328.

39 McCarthy, *Irishman*, p. 185.

40 Ibid., p. 198.

41 O'Connor, *Memoirs*, p. 70.

42 Brian M. Walker, *Parliamentary Election Results in Ireland, 1801–1922* (Dublin, 1978), pp. 118, 122.

43 McCarthy, *Reminiscences*, I, pp. 330–1.

44 *Freeman's Journal*, 28 Mar. 1879.

45 Ibid., 1 Apr. 1879.

46 Walker, *Parliamentary Election Results*, p. 122.

Chapter 3: *Vice-Chairman*

1 The two outgoing Home Rule candidates for Longford County, McCarthy and George Errington, were returned unopposed to parliament on 1 April 1880. See Walker, *Parliamentary Election Results*, p. 125.

2 *Freeman's Journal*, 18 May 1880.

3 McCarthy, *Reminiscences*, II, p. 179.

4 Justin McCarthy, *Modern Leaders* (New York, 1872), p. 126.

5 Justin McCarthy, *The Story of Gladstone's Life* (London, 1898).

6 Gladstone Papers, Add. MS 44412, f. 73: McCarthy to Gladstone, 16 Feb. 1867.

7 Ibid., Add. MS 44416, ff 215–16: McCarthy to Gladstone, 21 Nov. 1868.

8 For Mitchel on Gladstone and Bright, see also James Quinn, *John Mitchel* (Dublin, 2008), pp. 80–1.

9 Gladstone Papers, Add. MS 44459, f. 9: McCarthy to Gladstone, 3 Jan. 1879.

10 William O'Brien, *Recollections* (London, 1905), p. 255.

11 McCarthy, *Irishman*, p. 251.

12 Ibid.

13 Justin McCarthy and R. M. Praed, *Our Book of Memories: Letters of Justin McCarthy to Mrs Campbell Praed* (London, 1912), p. 2.

14 *Hansard*, 3rd series, cclii, 148–51 (20 May 1880).

15 E. J. Feuchtwanger, *Democracy and Empire: Britain, 1865–1914* (London, 1985), p. 150.

16 *Freeman's Journal*, 28 Dec. 1880.

17 F. S. L. Lyons, *Charles Stewart Parnell* (London, 1977), p. 144.

18 Extracts from review printed with the first volume of McCarthy's *A History of the Four Georges* (London, 1884).

19 Chamberlain to McCarthy, 30 Apr. 1882, quoted in R. Barry O'Brien, *The Life of Charles Stewart Parnell, 1846–1891* (2 vols, London, 1898), I, p. 342.

20 Parnell to W. O'Shea, 28 [actually 29] Apr. 1882, quoted in Robert Kee, *The Laurel and the Ivy: The Story of Charles Stewart Parnell and Irish Nationalism* (London, 1993), p. 431.

21 McCarthy, *Reminiscences*, I, p. 441.

22 Ibid., p. 439.

23 See articles such as 'The Common-Sense of Home Rule' (Mar. 1880) and 'Ireland in '48 and Ireland Now' (Dec. 1880).

24 McCarthy and Praed, *Our Book of Memories*, p. 1.

25 McCarthy to Praed, 2 Apr. 1890, quoted in ibid., p. 236.

26 K. Theodore Hoppen, *The Mid-Victorian Generation, 1846–1886* (Oxford, 1998), p. 675.

27 McCarthy, *Reminiscences*, II, p. 112.

28 Ibid., p. 113.

29 Eighty-five were returned for Irish constituencies, and one, T. P. O'Connor, was returned for the Scotland division of Liverpool.

30 Quoted in Conor Cruise O'Brien, *Parnell and His Party, 1880–90* (2nd edn, London, 1964), p. 143.

31 McCarthy to Praed, [25] Nov. 1885, quoted in McCarthy and Praed, *Our Book of Memories*, p. 26.

32 McCarthy to Praed, Nov. 1885, quoted in ibid., pp. 25–6.

33 See Walker, *Parliamentary Election Results*, p. 133.

34 See ibid., p. 134.

35 TNA, Carnarvon Papers, 30/6/67/32: 'Memo of conversation with J. McCarthy 13 Dec. 1885'. I am grateful to the Controller of Her Britannic Majesty's Stationery Office for permission to quote from this memorandum.

36   McCarthy, *Reminiscences*, II, p. 113.

37   McCarthy to Praed, Dec. 1885, quoted in McCarthy and Praed, *Our Book of Memories*, p. 28.

38   *Hansard*, 3rd series, CCCV, 1671–2 (21 May 1886).

39   McCarthy to Praed, 7 June 1886, quoted in McCarthy and Praed, *Our Book of Memories*, p. 40.

40   See Walker, *Parliamentary Election Results*, p. 139.

41   McCarthy to Praed, 6 July 1886, quoted in McCarthy and Praed, *Our Book of Memories*, p. 43.

42   See Walker, *Parliamentary Election Results*, p. 140.

43   D. A. Hamer, *Liberal Politics in the Age of Gladstone and Rosebery: A Study in Leadership and Policy* (London, 1972), p. 124.

44   McCarthy, *Irishman*, p. 290.

45   McCarthy to Praed, Oct. 1886, quoted in McCarthy and Praed, *Our Book of Memories*, p. 67.

46   McCarthy to Praed, 14 Feb. 1887, quoted in ibid., p. 81.

47   McCarthy to Praed, 2 Jan. 1887, quoted in ibid., p. 71.

48   Hoppen, *The Mid-Victorian Generation*, p. 645.

49   L. P. Curtis, jr, *Coercion and Conciliation in Ireland, 1880–1892: A Study in Conservative Unionism* (Princeton, 1963), p. 174.

50   McCarthy to Praed, July 1887, quoted in McCarthy and Praed, *Our Book of Memories*, p. 115.

51   For an amusing account of McCarthy sharing a platform in Gloucestershire with Arthur Brend Winterbotham, Liberal MP for Cirencester, see Raymond, *Portraits of the Nineties*, pp. 239–40. In late 1887 John Dillon also spent some time addressing meetings in England. (See F. S. L. Lyons, *John Dillon: A Biography* (London, 1968), p. 92.)

52   McCarthy to Praed, Apr. 1887, quoted in McCarthy and Praed, *Our Book of Memories*, p. 101.

53   McCarthy to Praed, May 1887, quoted in ibid., p. 107.

54   McCarthy to Praed, 25 Dec. 1888, quoted in ibid., p. 169.

55   McCarthy to Praed, Feb. 1890, quoted in ibid., p. 220.

56   McCarthy to Praed, Mar. 1888, quoted in ibid., p. 148.

57   McCarthy to Praed, 3 Apr. 1888, quoted in ibid., p. 150.

58   McCarthy to Praed, Apr. 1890, quoted in ibid., p. 239.

59   McCarthy to Praed, Aug. 1890, quoted in ibid., pp. 249–50.

60   See, for example, F. S. L. Lyons, *The Fall of Parnell, 1890–91* (London, 1960), pp. 72–149; O'Brien, *Parnell and His Party*, pp. 277–346; and Frank Callanan, *The Parnell Split, 1890–91* (Cork, 1992), pp. 9–53.

61   McCarthy to Praed, 16 Nov. 1890, quoted in McCarthy and Praed, *Our Book of Memories*, p. 255.

62   McCarthy to Praed, 1 Jan. 1890, quoted in ibid., p. 210.

63   Morley to Harcourt, 10 Nov. 1890, quoted in A. G. Gardiner, *The Life of Sir William Harcourt* (2 vols, London, 1923), II, p. 82.

64   Quoted in O'Brien, *Parnell and His Party*, p. 290.

65   See Richard Shannon, *Gladstone: Heroic Minister, 1865–1898* (London, 2000), p. 299.

66   John Morley, *The Life of William Ewart Gladstone* (3 vols, London, 1903), III, p. 436.

67   McCarthy to Praed, [24 Nov. 1890], quoted in McCarthy and Praed, *Our Book of Memories*, p. 258.

68   McCarthy and Praed, *Our Book of Memories*, p. 259.

69   John Viscount Morley, *Recollections* (2 vols, London, 1917), I, p. 261.

70   H. C. G. Matthew, *Gladstone, 1875–1898* (Oxford, 1995), p. 314.

71   Richard Shannon, *Gladstone: I: 1809–1865* (London, 1984), p. 161.

72   Quoted in ibid.

73   Quoted in ibid., p. 163.

74   Alvin Jackson, *Home Rule: An Irish History, 1800–2000* (London, 2003), p. 75.

75   See Morley, *Recollections*, I, 262.

76   McCarthy to Praed, 25 Nov. 1890, quoted in McCarthy and Praed, *Our Book of Memories*, p. 258.

77   McCarthy to Praed, [26 Nov. 1890], quoted in ibid., p. 259.

78   McCarthy to Praed, 28 Nov. 1890, quoted in ibid., p. 260.

79   Manifesto quoted in Lyons, *Fall of Parnell*, pp. 320–6.

80   O'Brien, *Parnell and His Party*, p. 312.

81   Patrick J. Walsh, *William J. Walsh, Archbishop of Dublin* (London, 1928), p. 416.

82   Quoted in Donal Sullivan, *The Story of Room 15* (Dublin, 1891), pp. 21–2.

83   Joseph Lee, *The Modernisation of Irish Society, 1848–1918* (Dublin, 1973), pp. 115–16.

84   Sullivan, *Story of Room 15*, p. 39.

85   Ibid., p. 43.

Chapter 4: *Reluctant Chairman*

1   *Freeman's Journal*, 11 Dec. 1890.

2   McCarthy to Praed, 17 Dec. 1890, quoted in McCarthy and Praed, *Our Book of Memories*, p. 271.

3   Quoted in Callanan, *The Parnell Split*, p. 70. (It has been suggested that Parnell 'borrowed' this phrase from Daniel O'Connell. See George W. E. Russell, *Portraits of the Seventies* (London, 1916), p. 21.)

4   McCarthy to Praed, 23 Dec. 1890, quoted in McCarthy and Praed, *Our Book of Memories*, p. 272.

5   McCarthy to Praed, 18 Feb. 1891, quoted in ibid., p. 282.

6   McCarthy to Healy, 12 Jan. 1891, quoted in T. M. Healy, *Letters and Leaders of My Day* (2 vols, London, 1928), I, p. 350.

7   Ibid.

8   McCarthy to Praed, [11] Feb. 1891, quoted in McCarthy and Praed, *Our Book of Memories*, p. 280.

9   McCarthy to Praed, 13 Feb. 1891, quoted in ibid., p. 281.

10 McCarthy to Praed, 17 Aug. 1891, quoted in ibid., p. 299. I am grateful to Gerard Doyle, to the Public Information & Enquiries Group, Bank of England, and to the Office for National Statistics, for the conversion factor.

11 I am again grateful to Gerard Doyle, to the Bank, and to the Office, for the conversion factor.

12 McCarthy to Praed, 7 Oct. 1891, quoted in McCarthy and Praed, *Our Book of Memories*, p. 301.

13 O'Brien, *Recollections*, pp. 257–8.

14 Ibid., p. 258.

15 McCarthy, *Reminiscences*, II, p. 89.

16 McCarthy to Praed, 7 Oct. 1891, quoted in McCarthy and Praed, *Our Book of Memories*, p. 302.

17 McCarthy to Praed, 11 Mar. 1892, quoted in ibid., p. 312.

18 The re-election of T. P. O'Connor in Liverpool brought the number of Irish Party seats up to 72.

19 Sir John Ross, *The Years of My Pilgrimage: Random Reminiscences* (London, 1924), pp. 64, 66. I am grateful to Alvin Jackson for this reference.

20 See Walker, *Parliamentary Election Results*, p. 147.

21 Ibid.

22 See G. R. Searle, *A New England? Peace and War, 1886–1918* (Oxford, 2004), p. 862.

23 Quoted in ibid., p. 163.

24 Quoted in Jackson, *Home Rule*, pp. 81–2.

25 McCarthy to Praed, 8 Feb. 1893, quoted in McCarthy and Praed, *Our Book of Memories*, p. 352.

26 *Hansard*, 4th series, VIII, 976–7 (9 Feb. 1893).

27 Justin McCarthy, 'The Home Rule Bill', *Nineteenth Century*, XXXIII (Mar. 1893), pp. 369–74.

28   *Hansard*, 4th series, x, 1860–1 (10 Apr. 1893).

29   Ibid., 1862.

30   Ibid., 1862–3.

31   Patrick Buckland, *Irish Unionism: One. The Anglo-Irish and the New Ireland 1885–1922* (Dublin, 1972), pp. 9–10.

32   *Hansard*, 4th series, xv, 574 (10 May 1893).

33   Ibid., 575–6.

34   Ibid., 575.

35   Harold Spender, *The Story of the Home Rule Session, reprinted . . . from 'The Westminster Gazette'* (London, 1893), pp. 59–61.

36   McCarthy to Praed, 27 July 1893, quoted in McCarthy and Praed, *Our Book of Memories*, p. 365.

37   See Andrew Roberts, *Salisbury: Victorian Titan* (London, 2000), p. 588.

38   Alvin Jackson, *Colonel Edward Saunderson: Land and Loyalty in Victorian Ireland* (Oxford, 1995), p. 3.

39   McCarthy, *Reminiscences*, II, pp. 395–7.

40   Roberts, *Salisbury*, pp. 1–2, 14–15, 572.

41   Ibid., p. 586.

42   Quoted in ibid., p. 586.

43   See ibid., p. 587.

44   See Searle, *A New England?*, p. 151.

45   *Hansard*, 4th series, xvi, 1741–3 (1 Sept. 1893).

46   Ibid., 1744.

47   Alvin Jackson, *Ireland 1798–1998: War, Peace and Beyond* (2nd edn, Chichester, 2010), p. 221.

48   R. C. K. Ensor, *England, 1870–1914* (Oxford, 1936), pp. 211–12.

49   Quoted in Robert Rhodes James, *Rosebery: A Biography of Archibald Philip, Fifth Earl of Rosebery* (London, 1963), p. 335.

50   McCarthy to Praed, 17 July 1895, quoted in McCarthy and Praed, *Our Book of Memories*, p. 401.

51   F. S. L. Lyons, 'The machinery of the Irish Parliamentary Party in the general election of 1895', *Irish Historical Studies*, VIII: no. 30 (Sept. 1952), p. 138.

52   McCarthy and Praed, *Our Book of Memories*, pp. 329–30 (notes made by Praed of a conversation with McCarthy on 23 August 1892).

53   Lyons, *Dillon*, p. 152.

54   Quoted in McCarthy and Praed, *Our Book of Memories*, p. 372.

55   See below, p. 80.

56   See above, p. 30.

57   Raymond, *Portraits of the Nineties*, p. 246.

58 O'Brien, *Recollections*, pp. 256–7.

59 McCarthy to Praed, 17 May 1892, quoted in McCarthy and Praed, *Our Book of Memories*, pp. 314–15.

60 McCarthy to Praed, 10 June 1893, quoted in ibid., p. 362.

61 McCarthy to Praed, 16 Mar. 1894, quoted in ibid., p. 377.

62 McCarthy to Praed, 18 Apr. 1894, quoted in ibid., p. 378.

63 Quoted in Margaret A. Banks, *Edward Blake, Irish Nationalist: A Canadian Statesman in Irish Politics, 1892–1907* (Toronto, 1957), pp. 90–1.

64 McCarthy to Praed, 10 Sept. 1894, quoted in McCarthy and Praed, *Our Book of Memories*, p. 383.

65 Blake to T. P. O'Connor, 3 Oct. 1894, quoted in Banks, *Edward Blake*, p. 96.

66 Quoted in Lyons, 'Machinery of the Irish Parliamentary Party . . . 1895', pp. 123–4.

67 Lyons, *Dillon*, p. 166.

68 Quoted in Banks, *Edward Blake*, pp. 115, 126–7.

69 Quoted in Lyons, 'Machinery of the Irish Parliamentary Party . . . 1895', p. 132.

70 See Walker, *Parliamentary Election Results*, p. 154.

71 See Thomas J. Morrissey, *William Martin Murphy* (Dublin, 2011), p. 29.

72 *Freeman's Journal*, 2 Sept. 1895.

73 Granville to Gladstone, 21 Jan. 1891, quoted in Lyons, *Fall of Parnell*, pp. 231–2.

74 McCarthy to Praed, [11] Feb. 1891, quoted in McCarthy and Praed, *Our Book of Memories*, p. 280.

75 McCarthy to Praed, Apr. 1891, quoted in ibid., p. 290.

76 McCarthy to Praed, 23 Apr. 1891, quoted in ibid., p. 290.

77 Lyons, *Dillon*, p. 140.

78 McCarthy to Praed, 15 Mar. 1891, quoted in McCarthy and Praed, *Our Book of Memories*, p. 286.

79 Ibid., p. 287.

80 McCarthy to Praed, May 1892, quoted in ibid., p. 313.

81 McCarthy to Praed, 28 Aug. 1894, quoted in ibid., p. 383.

82 McCarthy to Praed, 8 Dec. 1892, quoted in ibid., p. 336.

83 McCarthy to Praed, 21 Nov. 1894, quoted in ibid., p. 389.

84 McCarthy to Praed, 16 Feb. 1895, quoted in ibid., p. 392.

85 See above, pp. 33–4.

86 McCarthy to Praed, 28 June 1895, quoted in McCarthy and Praed, *Our Book of Memories*, pp. 400–1.

87 Quoted in Lyons, *Dillon*, p. 170.

88 Ibid.

89 McCarthy to Praed, 7 Feb. 1896, quoted in ibid., p. 407.

90 McCarthy to Praed, 29 May 1896, quoted in ibid., p. 411.

91 McCarthy to Praed, 31 Dec. 1897, quoted in ibid., p. 421.

92 McCarthy to Praed, 14 Nov. 1911, quoted in ibid., p. 445.

93 McCarthy to Praed, 22 June 1901, quoted in ibid., p. 428.

94 See R. F. Foster, *W. B. Yeats: A Life. I: The Apprentice Mage, 1865–1914* (Oxford, 1997), pp. 425, 428.

Conclusion

1 Searle, *A New England?*, p. 149.

2 See e.g. Lyons, *Dillon*, p. 152, and Paul Bew, *Enigma: A New Life of Charles Stewart Parnell* (Dublin, 2011), p. 169.

3 Russell, *Portraits of the Seventies*, p. 15.

4 Ibid., p. 22.

5 Quoted in O'Brien, *Recollections*, pp. 255–6.

6 Ibid., p. 256.

7 Jackson, *Ireland 1798–1998*, p. 123.

8 O'Brien, *Recollections*, p. 257.

Select Bibliography

The main sources of biographical material on McCarthy are his own writings, especially his *Reminiscences* (2 vols, London, 1899), *The Story of an Irishman* (London, 1904), and *Irish Recollections* (London, 1911). His letters to Rosa Praed, printed in Justin McCarthy and R. M. Praed, *Our Book of Memories: Letters of Justin McCarthy to Mrs Campbell Praed* (London, 1912), are also indispensable.

Additional material can be found in McCarthy's *Portraits of the Sixties* (London, 1903) and *British Political Leaders* (London, 1903). As an example of his historical writing, see *A History of Our Own Times* (7 vols, London, 1878–1905).

For a selection of essays on McCarthy, see George W. E. Russell, *Portraits of the Seventies* (London, 1916), pp. 15–24; E. T. Raymond, *Portraits of the Nineties* (London, 1921), pp. 239–47; S. L. Gwynn, rev. Alan O'Day, 'McCarthy, Justin (1830–1912)' in H. C. G. Matthew and Brian Harrison (eds), *Oxford Dictionary of National Biography* (Oxford, 2004), vol. 35, pp. 112–14; and Alan O'Day, 'McCarthy, Justin' in James McGuire and James Quinn (eds), *Dictionary of Irish Biography* (Cambridge, 2009), vol. 5, pp. 807–9.

Those studying McCarthy's time as an MP can still benefit greatly from reading the works of F. S. L. Lyons. See especially his *The Irish Parliamentary Party, 1890–1910* (London, 1951), *The Fall of Parnell, 1890–91* (London, 1960), *John Dillon: A Biography* (London, 1968), and *Charles Stewart Parnell* (London, 1977). Conor Cruise O'Brien's *Parnell and His Party, 1880–90* (2nd edn, Oxford, 1964) has been heavily used in chapter 3.

McCarthy's entire life was lived during the time Ireland was part of the United Kingdom of Great Britain and Ireland. Recent surveys of this period in Irish history include two volumes by Alvin Jackson: *Home Rule: An Irish History, 1800–2000* (London, 2003) and *Ireland 1798–1998: War, Peace and Beyond* (2nd edn, Chichester, 2010); and Paul Bew, *Ireland: The Politics of Enmity, 1789–2006* (Oxford, 2007).

McCarthy spent most of his life in England. Initially as a journalist, and subsequently as a politician, he was immersed in British politics. It is therefore necessary to see him in a British context. Useful general texts for this purpose include K. Theodore Hoppen, *The Mid-Victorian Generation, 1846–1886* (Oxford, 1998) and G. R. Searle, *A New England? Peace and War, 1886–1918* (Oxford, 2004). Alan J. Lee's *The Origins of the Popular Press in England, 1855–1914* (London, 1976) provides a detailed background to McCarthy's professional career, as does Stephen Koss's *The Rise and Fall of the Political Press in Britain* (London, 1990).

Many of McCarthy's contemporaries in the Irish Party wrote their memoirs. See in particular William O'Brien, *Recollections* (London, 1905) and *Evening Memories* (London, 1920); T. M. Healy, *Letters and Leaders of My Day* (2 vols, London, 1928); and T. P. O'Connor, *Memoirs of an Old Parliamentarian* (2 vols, London, 1929). Two volumes in this HAI Life and Times New Series give interesting perspectives on political figures whose careers coincided with that of McCarthy: Carla King, *Michael Davitt* (Dublin, 2009) and Thomas J. Morrissey, *William Martin Murphy* (Dublin, 2011). See also Frank Callanan, *T. M. Healy* (Cork, 1996) and Paul Bew, *Enigma: A New Life of Charles Stewart Parnell* (Dublin, 2011).

Of the numerous biographies of Gladstone, see especially John Morley, *The Life of William Ewart Gladstone* (3 vols, London, 1903); Richard Shannon, *Gladstone, I, 1809–1865* (London, 1984) and *Gladstone: Heroic Minister, 1865–1898* (London, 2000); and H. C. G. Matthew, *Gladstone, 1875–1898* (Oxford, 1995). For an alternative perspective on Home Rule and related issues, see Alvin Jackson, *Colonel Edward Saunderson: Land and Loyalty in Victorian Ireland* (Oxford, 1995) and Andrew Roberts, *Salisbury: Victorian Titan* (London, 2000).

Studies that give a wider perspective on issues relevant to McCarthy's life include James Loughlin, *Gladstone, Home Rule and the Ulster Question, 1882–93* (Dublin, 1986); Alvin Jackson, *The Ulster Party: Irish Unionists in the House of Commons, 1884–1911* (Oxford, 1989); Frank Callanan, *The Parnell Split, 1890–91* (Cork, 1992); and Patrick Maume, *The Long Gestation: Irish Nationalist Life, 1891–1918* (Dublin, 1999). Articles and other books found to be particularly useful are cited in the notes.

Index